10/10

MONAI

MONARCHY

A SERIES OF PAPERS
DELIVERED TO THE TEMENOS ACADEMY
PUBLISHED TO MARK THE GOLDEN JUBILEE OF
HER MAJESTY QUEEN ELIZABETH II

JOHN S. ALLITT

L. L. BLAKE

JOHN CAREY

GREVEL LINDOP

JOSEPH MILNE

KATHLEEN RAINE

TEMENOS ACADEMY

TEMENOS ACADEMY PAPERS NO. 18

These papers were given at the Temenos Academy during the summer of 2002,
with the exception of the paper by Grevel Lindop
which was given at the Temenos Academy in April 2001.

First published 2002 by
The Temenos Academy
19–22 Charlotte Road
London EC2A 3SG, UK

Registered Charity No. 1043015

Typeset by Colin Etheridge

Printed at
Smith Settle, Otley

Our thanks to all those who have contributed to this volume,
particularly the many subscribers who have made this publication possible,
and whose names are listed at the back.

CONTENTS

MONARCHY

A SERIES OF PAPERS

MONARCHY & THE IMAGINATION

Kings and queens, princes and princesses belong, above all, to the proper disposal of things in the world of fairy-tales, the universal once-upon-a-time of the imagination of humankind from time immemorial. Whether in Ireland's rain, Russia's snows, Norway's long winter nights or India's monsoon, the stories are told and have raised their imagined palaces and established their enduring kingdoms of which all the world's childhood are citizens, and of which we have all been inhabitants. Are these kings and queens memories of history become legendary, as the euhemerists would have us believe? Or does history forever seek to realise dream? There are passages in Gibbon's *The Decline and Fall of the Roman Empire* describing the City of Byzantium which might come from some fairy-tale. Gibbon thus describes the imperial splendour:

> The square before the sigma was decorated by a fountain, and the margin of the bason was lined and encompassed with plates of silver. In the beginning of each season this bason instead of water was replenished with the most exquisite fruits, which were abandoned to the populace for the entertainment of the Prince. He enjoyed this tumultuous spectacle from a throne resplendent with gold and gems which was raised by a marble staircase to the height of a lofty terrace. Below the throne were seated the officers of his guards, the magistrates, the chiefs of the factions of the circus; the inferior steps were occupied by the people, and the place below was covered with troops of dancers, singers and pantomimes.

We have to remember that Constantine the Great built Byzantium in the likeness of the City of Jerusalem as imagined in the Book of

Revelation, and Justinian restored Santa Sophia in emulation of the temple of Jerusalem—did not the city itself embody that age-old dream? Gibbon himself scorned the fantasy of:

> . . . a golden tree, with its leaves and branches that sheltered a multitude of birds, that warbled their artificial notes, and two lions of massy gold, and of the natural size who looked and roared like their brothers in the forest . . .

That Golden Tree has made its way back into poetry in Yeats's poem 'Sailing to Byzantium':

> Once out of nature I shall never take
> My bodily form from any natural thing,
> But such a form as Grecian goldsmiths make
> Of hammered gold and gold enamelling
> To keep a drowsy Emperor awake;
> Or set upon a golden bough to sing
> To lords and ladies of Byzantium
> Of what is past, or passing, or to come.

Commenting on Lady Gregory's *Gods and Fighting Men* Yeats brings that country of the Imagination full circle when he writes:

> . . . The poor fisher has no possessions of the world and so no responsibility for it, and if he dreams of a love-gift better than the brown shawl that seems too common for poetry, why should he not dream of a glove made of the skin of a bird, or shoes made from the skin of a fish, or a coat made from the glittering garment of the salmon? Was it not Aeschylus who said he but served up dishes from the banquet of Homer, but Homer himself found the great banquet on an earthen floor and under a broken roof.

In the same foreword he writes:

I have read in a fabulous book that Adam had but to imagine a bird and it was born into life, and that he created all things out of himself by nothing more important than an unflagging fancy.

How else are cities built but according to a model 'laid up in Heaven' of the city of the Imagination?

In that kingdom of 'once-upon-a-time' kings have unlimited power and splendour, secure kingdoms and loyal subjects. Princes are handsome and courteous to all, to the poor and the old no less than to personages of the highest rank. Princesses are beautiful, and set a high price on themselves, some hard task to be performed as the condition of marriage; and their hand may be won by the third son of a poor woodcutter or the chosen friend of Puss-in-Boots as easily as by Lohengrin from a mysterious high world. In the world of imagination there are no Presidents or Prime Ministers; and do we not in the Lord's Prayer attribute to God 'the Kingdom, the Power and the Glory'?

*

As for King George, the 'real' King, his neat bearded profile was familiar because it appeared on our postage-stamps (red penny stamps for letters, green halfpenny stamps for post-cards), and was part of the natural order of things, like the weather. King George and Queen Mary lived, by no means in the *mundus imaginalis* but at least in a world apart from the rest of us, in a palace, and invisible except on special occasions—the opening of buildings, inspecting troops, launching liners—that brought them into public view.

King George visited our obscure East-London suburb on the occasion of his opening the hospital, named after him, and we school children lined the streets of Ilford to be rewarded by a glimpse of the King and Queen as they drove past in an open car. The occasion was of importance mainly to grown-ups involved in the important event in one way or another. Even so there was a general feeling that a little gold-dust had been scattered from that passing car—some magical power still belonged, it seems, to 'real' kings and queens, or to princes, as in the popular song 'I know a girl, who knows a girl, who danced with the Prince of Wales'—a popular figure at that time.

*

Monarchy has, with Shakespeare, remained within the realm of poetry. Shakespeare was by profession employed with his company of players by Queen Elizabeth I and was therefore bound to support the Tudor monarchy. A whole paper—many papers—could be devoted to Shakespeare's historical plays, which are, in a sense, the foundation of the English concept of Kingship; but it is not only in these that the theme of monarchy predominates. In *Macbeth*, *Hamlet*, *King Lear*, *A Midsummer Night's Dream* and *As You Like It*, kingship and its legitimacy are dominant themes. In *A Midsummer Night's Dream* the magnanimous conduct of Duke Theseus towards the 'rude mechanicals' who offered their play for his entertainment is contrasted with the contempt of Philostrate, the 'master of revels' and with Hippolyta, his bride-to-be's frank boredom. In *As You Like It*, the rightful Duke, banished by his usurping brother, sets up his court in the Forest of Arden, where his authority is in harmony with the order of nature, where he

> Finds tongues in trees, books in the running brooks,
> Sermons in stones, and good in everything.
>
> (II.i)

In *King Lear* Kent (banished and in disguise) names a quality in the King (though stripped of his rank) that entitles him to his service:

Attendant How now! What art thou?
Kent A man, sir.
Lear What dost thou profess? What wouldst thou with us?
Kent I do profess no less than I seem: to serve him truly that will put me in trust; to love him that is honest; to converse with him that is wise and says little; to fear judgement; to fight

when I cannot chose; and to eat no fish.

Lear   What art thou?

Kent   A very honest hearted fellow, and as poor as the King.

Lear   If thou be as poor for a subject as he is for a King, thou art poor enough. What wouldst thou?

Kent   Service.

Lear   Whom wouldst thou serve?

Kent   You.

Lear   Dost thou know me, fellow?

Kent   No sir; but you have that in your countenance which I would fain call master.

Lear   What is that?

Kent   Authority.

(I.iv)

Later in the play Lear himself justifies the respect for the invisible honour of rank, at the moment when he himself has been stripped of his following of a hundred knights:

Lear   O! Reason not the need; our basest beggars
       are in the poorest thing superfluous:
       Allow not nature more than nature needs
       Man's life is cheap as beasts'. Thou art a lady;
       If only to go warm were gorgeous,
       Why, nature needs not what thou gorgeous wearest,
       Which scarcely keeps thee warm. But, for true need,—
       You see me here, you gods, a poor old man,
       As full of grief as age; wretched in both!

(II.iv)

In contrast with the authority Kent sees in Lear, though stripped of his power, Macbeth's usurped authority brings him neither happiness nor honour; whereas Banquo, 'Less happy than Macbeth, yet happier', will be honoured as fathering a line of kings. For Shakespeare, kingship represented the fitting order of things, to which it was for actual kings to conform.

*

After the reign of Elizabeth I fact and imagination in history tended to diverge. Mary Queen of Scots captured the imagination but lost her kingdom. In the Civil War a generation later, Cromwell was victorious, and King Charles I's claim to the 'divine right of kings' rejected by the nation. Arguably the King overstepped the bounds of natural justice; but Cromwell's victory was short-lived, and the office of Lord Protector soon expired. He proved to be a tyrant whose reign is remembered in Ireland as 'the curse of Cromwell'. The nation felt happier with a king, and with the restoration of Charles II the absolute power of the King's 'divine right' was curbed by Parliament in a 'constitutional monarchy' which has lasted ever since.

Poetry again returned with power in the attempt to restore the Stuart Monarchy by the 'young Pretender', Charles Edward Stuart. The political battle was lost, but the songs of the 'Forty-five' testify to this day to the victory of 'bonnie Prince Charlie' of the Scottish Royalists as the uncrowned King of Scotland: 'Follow thee! Follow thee! Wha wadna follow thee! King o' oor hieland hearts, bonnie Prince Charlie!' In fact Prince Charles Edward fell short of the image poetry has created of him, but remains as a legend as 'the King ower the water', who holds Scotland's loyalty almost to this day, with Wallace and Bruce, in the songs that live on. However, the Scottish tongue has a gift for scorn and denigration no less than its eloquence for patriotism, but less appreciated on the English side of the border, where the Hanoverian Monarchy was greeted with songs of a different kind, like: 'Wha the diel hae we gotten for a King/ But a wee wee German lairdie!'

*

In the course of the twentieth Century the world as we know it has been transformed by technology. At the end of the First World War, radio sets consisted of a piece of quartz and a 'cat's whisker' with which one had to find the active spot, and could then with a pair of ear-phones listen to the voice of 'London calling'. Now the media of radio and television can project the same programme into as many receiving sets as can be manufactured and sold. The result is that party politics and political personalities have become our daily entertainment. That egalitarian democracy should have become the accepted norm of the social structure of the modern West (and rapidly spreading to the rest of the world) can be seen as the inevitable outcome of this technological revolution. We are encouraged by tricks of technique to imagine that these personalities who enter our living-rooms through the television screens are our personal acquaintances, since they have access to our private rooms at all times. As a rule they choose to be known by abbreviated first names formerly used among friends. Plato, who held democracy in low regard, noted that people like it because it allows everyone to do whatever they like, but warns that it leads to tyranny. This is a danger we can see for ourselves in the concentration of power in the hands of whoever controls the Press and the Media—the likes of Rupert Murdoch or the late Robert Maxwell—able to control the minds of multitudes of people not in a position to question whatever information, true or false, the media disseminate. Thus the authority of national institutions is imperceptibly undermined. Those who control the media can destroy political figures and institutions and communicate to the nation an attitude of cynical doubt about what is sneeringly described as 'the establishment'.

Monarchy is of course threatened by this universal demoticisation of public life. All values are eroded by the habit of mind that supposes that whatever a majority chooses must be right or can be decided by a general election: but values have their roots elsewhere than in majority decisions. Never the less monarchy is protected by the very fact that it is not a political office like that of an elected president or prime minister.

This country remains an officially Christian country, a fact that has deep roots and a reality still reflected in many aspects of our national life. The sacred is an order of things that belongs not to the world of technology and science but to inner realities of the mind, immeasurable values and meanings on which human civilizations have been built from the beginning. It is for this reason that I find myself a supporter of monarchy as the best safeguard of human values. Just because the foundation of monarchy is not political it safeguards those human freedoms and values which are the marks of true civilisation.

Americans may sing 'God Bless America' but this has no relevance to the American Constitution or the office of President as such, which is purely secular. Vocal sections of our press and media might like to see this country become a republic, but it would be hard to see what we would gain thereby, and all too easy to see what we would lose.

Since the restoration of the Monarchy in the person of King Charles II, the performance of the ceremony of coronation by a priest of the Church of England in the person of the Archbishop of Canterbury confers on the anointed king or queen a spiritual authority as head of the Church of England. The reigning monarch is under the Law, and under God, but head of the Church of England whose independence from Rome was established by Henry VIII at the time of the Reformation. L. L. Blake, the constitutional historian, has explained in detail the nature and implications of this constitutional fact. Since most of the offices performed by both political and royal figures are purely secular in their nature there are no doubt at the Palace advisers engaged in projecting this secular and democratically acceptable image of royalty. This is natural enough but does never the less lessen the respect in which monarchy is held.

This probably means nothing to a great number of people who 'do not believe in God.' But the existence of divinity does not depend on belief or disbelief of a majority, or on a general election. In this context I would like to challenge the authority assumed by disbelief in the words of our national prophet, William Blake:

> Did Jesu teach doubt—or did he
> Give any lessons in Philosophy?
> Charge visionaries with deceiving,

Or call men wise for not believing?
('The Everlasting Gospel', Keynes 756)

Neither does the office depend on the personal faith of the monarch. Queen Victoria accepted her office with the famous words 'I will be good'. On the whole no doubt she was, and we may be the better for a monarch who is 'good' and sets a good example to the rest of us. No doubt Queen Elizabeth II has done so, and in the face of great difficulties. But the royal office belongs to the national identity, not to the personality of the monarch. In the same way, in the administration of the Law, the Judge, when he dons the wig that signifies his office, is no longer a private person, but personifies the Law, in whose name he gives judgment.

*

The nature of the royal office is imprinted on the coin of the realm. The letters 'FD', or 'Fid. Def.' stand for 'Fidei Defensor' usually translated as 'Defender of the Faith'—that is to say the Church of England. It is a pity that the nature and history of our constitution is scarcely taught at all in our schools, and is a matter of general ignorance and indifference.

Our Prince of Wales, in an important speech, has given a wider meaning to the words (perfectly consistent with the latin) in expressing his wish, if he becomes King, to be known not as 'Defender of the Faith' but as 'Defender of Faith'. Thus the royal title would include not only Catholics, Non-Conformists and Jews, but important communities of Muslims, Hindus, Jains, Sikhs, Buddhists, and other non-Christian ethnic groups who now enjoy British citizenship; not to mention many people who belong to no religious community but who have in their hearts the love of the divine Being. Not only must these words give enormous hope and protection: the Prince's words are in themselves a powerful statement against racism.

Thus in our national life the monarch is the shared symbol of a sacred authority above politics or personal power of whatever kind. What it does for the nation is to affirm that not man but God is supreme. However, welcome as are the Prince's words, it never the less remains true that England is officially a Christian country whose Church is 'by law established'. By that authority certain offices of state—notably the coronation of the monarch—are carried out. One would not wish to see these constitutional structures undermined. These are collective and national, not personal and private, matters.

However, the supreme power in our modern secular democracies is clearly money. No candidate for the American presidency can present himself unless some powerful person or organisation puts up a very large sum of money. This compromises the freedom of any elected President from the start. In England this is not so, and any responsible candidate sponsored by his (or her) political party, can stand as a candidate. The reason for this is, without question, the supremacy of the Crown: the fact that we all are, constitutionally speaking 'Her Majesty's Subjects', and that the Queen presides over the opening of Parliament, protects a very precious freedom from subjugation by the all but supreme power of Mammon. The Murdochs and the Maxwells may control the media which is bad enough—but they do not control the Crown. The election of our Members of Parliament is as relatively free from the control of money as it is thanks to the Monarchy which sets a bound to the power of the Maxwells and the Murdochs. We are probably not as grateful as we should be, largely owing to the widespread ignorance as to how things work in our extremely complex constitutional monarchy, or to what extent our individual freedoms are guaranteed and underpinned by the Constitution.

*

Royalty is, in its ultimate nature, an archetype. Plato introduced this word, which has been given new actuality as a psychological fact by C.G. Jung in the twentieth century. As such, it is not the prerogative of any individual, monarch or commoner, but a universal human attribute, of which the monarch stands as a unifying symbol in relation to a particular nation. So understood, kingship is manhood in its fullest development, and queenship womanhood in its fullest development—by no means the same thing as political feminism. Kingship and queenship are used as terms signifying such perfection often in a purely poetic sense—one thinks of Shelley's 'Prince Athanase' or, in republican France, de Nerval's 'Prince d'Aquitaine a sa tour abolie'. William Blake, no royalist, wrote of himself as 'I, William Blake, a Mental Prince' ('Public Address', Keynes 599). Kingship is a quality of being, and again Blake defines this quality, in a letter to his old friend George Cumberland written shortly before his own death:

> Flaxman is gone and we must all soon follow, everyone to his Own Eternal House, leaving the Delusive Goddess Nature and her laws to get into Freedom from all Law of the Members into The Mind, in which every one is King and Priest in his own House. God send it so on Earth as it is in Heaven.
>
> (April 12th 1827)

In the Jewish tradition that every man is King and priest in his own household is acknowledged in the custom of the head of the household every Friday night (the Jewish holy day) dressing in his best clothes, and receiving respectful homage from younger members of the family. In Spain this custom was used to track down nominal Christian converts who were in reality still practising the Jewish religion, at the risk of life itself. (Blake could conceivably have known of this custom, highly as he himself regarded the Jews). Thus kingship is itself the highest attainment of humankind, reached by few; but perhaps we all know or have known some who have possessed the qualities of kingship, and, thereby, what Kent recognised in King Lear, 'authority'.

This concept of innate stature and rank is the basis of the caste system, which has prevailed in India, grounded as it is in human nature. There are four main castes, with many sub-divisions, essentially related to social functions. The highest caste is that of the Brahmins, who are custodians of spiritual knowledge, and of learning which in India is always related to spiritual knowledge in some form. Brahmins may not seek wealth or power and their authority is not political. The ruling caste, the Ksh-treyas, have the duty to support the Brahmins. Thus kings take second place in the order of things, a fact implicit in the coronation of our kings being conferred by Christian priesthood. Farmers, craftsmen, merchants and all the multitude of makers and doers who have made India a land of beauty and abundance are the Vaishyans, while the fourth caste, the Shudras, are the workmen. All four castes are essential to the prosperity of society as a whole, and with ups and downs the caste system has sustained India over many millennia. As indeed the class structure has served England well.

In the twentieth century we have seen the fourfold nature of humankind reaffirmed in the strongest possible psychological terms by C. G. Jung, as the four types of men, governed respectively by reason, feeling, sensation and intuition. The four apocalyptic beasts, eagle, lion, ox and angel (or man) establish the quaternity at the very heart of Christendom, and there are comparable mythological quaternities in most known cultures, past and present. People fall naturally into one or another of Jung's 'types', with, again, recognisable variations. Any human community—a colony for example—will form itself naturally into this pattern. The *Bhagavad Gītā* warns against the adoption of roles or tasks that are not proper to our natures, and we can see for ourselves that people are happiest when performing the work natural to them. Much of the unhappiness within our egalitarian democracies comes from our assumption that everyone should be everything at once. Or so it can be argued. In this imperfect world no system, no institution, is perfect, but monarchy, as an archetype, seems to correspond to something in human nature which has served this country very well. It is not the material and measurable that makes a nation but its ideas and values. The same is true for every individual life, and in the world of Imagination kings and queens, princes and princesses have, from time immemorial to the present day, designated those timeless, unageing values.

I began this paper by pointing out that monarchy is the unquestioned order of Fairyland, of which we have all been inhabitants. That is to say, monarchy is a powerful and enduring archetype. In confirmation of this view I would like to conclude by speaking of a work of imagination that has enchanted the late twentieth century, J. R. R. Tolkein's *The Lord of the Rings*. This imaginative narrative swept the campuses of America (and of England too) when it first appeared in 1955, and has been given new popularity as a brilliant film in 2002. The author was a distinguished professor of linguistics in Oxford, member of the academic circle known as 'The Inklings', which included C. S. Lewis, Charles Williams, and other members of Oxford's elite. He was in religion a professed Catholic: as far as civilisation has brought the western world from the traditional sources of myth and folklore. *The Lord of the Rings* is a major work that has been compared to Spenser's *Faerie Queene*, to Malory, and (by C. S. Lewis) to Ariosto. It is an imaginary world unrivalled in its relevance to the actual human situation 'comic, homely, epic, monstrous or diabolic' (Lewis's words). The third and final volume of this astonishing book is entitled *The Return of the King*, a figure whose anonymous presence throughout has come to represent honour, nobility, stability and peace, banishing the powers of evil and restoring justice, joy and due order throughout the world. Not only does the king banish and replace the rule of evil in the world but the 'stewardship' of rulers who have exercised their office justly on the whole, although the last holder of office dies rather than relinquish his power. His son, however, willingly hands it over and acknowledges the rightful king. The broken sword is mended, the dead tree lives again, and joy returns to the kingdom. Who does not feel, at the end of Tolkein's three volumes, that this is as it should be?

To a generation bereft of any shared religious *mythos*, this spacious imaginative work offers a world both comprehensive and satisfying. In that world the celestial hierarchies are represented by non-human races as are the hells and their evil populace. Within that world the 'hobbits', 'halflings' or little people may be entrusted with a task on whose fulfilment all the hierarchies depend—a reassuring message for a generation wondering what such small creatures as ourselves can do in a vast mysterious universe. It must be remembered that kingship is attributed to Jesus Christ, Christ the King, son of the heavenly Father who is 'King of Kings and Lord of Lords'. The Lord of the Rings has indeed restored due order to the modern Western imagination, and The Return of the King is more than a fictional fancy in a world starved of beauty and dignity, seeking for meaning in times that have lost their significance. It is a work of healing. In this archetypal masterpiece and in its resolution in The Return of the King due order is indeed restored to the mundus imaginalis.

You may rightly be wondering why I have not already mentioned the supreme archetypal king of England—King Arthur, half-legendary half-historic monarch who held court at Camelot, and who, mortally wounded in his last battle with his rebellious nephew did not die, but lies sleeping in a cave in Northumberland, or Wales, or elsewhere so the local legends say, and will come again with his knights when the nation's need is greatest. A greater writer than Tolkein, David Jones, has commemorated this myth in his poem The Sleeping Lord, with which I will conclude this paper:

Yet he sleeps on
                    very deep is his slumber:
how long has he been the sleeping lord?
Are the clammy ferns
                         his rustling vallance
does the buried rowan
                          ward him from evil, or
does he ward the tanglewood
                              and the denizens of the wood -
are the stunted oaks his gnarled guard
                            or are their knarred limbs
strong with his sap?
Do the small black horses
                           grass on the hunch of his shoulders?

Are the hills his couch
                or is he the couchant hills?
Are the slumbering valleys
                  him in slumber
                  are the still undulations
the still limbs of him sleeping?
Is the configuration of the land
                  the furrowed body of the lord—
are the scarred ridges
              his dented greaves -
do the trickling gullies
              yet drain his hog wounds?
Does the land wait the sleeping lord
              or is the wasted land
that very lord who sleeps?
                (from *The Sleeping Lord* by David Jones)

L. L. BLAKE

IN PRAISE OF THE QUEEN'S MAJESTY

This word 'Majesty'. It moves serenely and in the heart of the word is a great light: the Majaajyotish of Sanskrit, from which so many of our words are derived. 'Having great splendour' is the translation. Or, in Milton's words, 'That far-beaming blaze of Majesty'. Commentators on coronations have written about this light being present at the time of consecration of the king or queen to the service of the nation and commonwealth.

It was said about King George V:

> [He] was a religious man: for him this ancient ritual was an act of dedication. The blare of trumpets, the salvos of artillery, the archaic ceremony, the swell of anthems, the jewelled emblems, the hierophantic vestments in which he was successively arrayed, even the thin shafts of sunlight falling upon the fawn and azure hangings, upon the lords and prelates as they passed and re-passed across the blue carpet in their robes of scarlet, ermine and gold: all this was no more than an almost unrealised background to the sacred fact that he was being consecrated to the service of his peoples, to whom, kneeling alone before the altar, he had sworn a grave oath.[1]

But this light is in everyone, the light of majesty, otherwise we would not recognise it. The divine light which gives us essence and being. The Queen touched on it in her Christmas address of 2000: 'Whether we believe in God or not, I think most of us have a sense of the spiritual, that recognition of a deeper meaning and purpose in our lives, and I believe this sense flourishes despite the pressures of our world.' The light is there in all of us but in kings and queens it shines brightly at the time of coronation so that we are aware of its magnificence. 'That was the true Light, which lighteth every man that cometh into the world' says St John. We may call that light the Self. The *Kaṭha Upaniṣad* says:

> Self rides in the chariot of the body, intellect the firm-footed charioteer, discursive mind the reins.
> Senses are the horses, objects of desire the roads. When Self is joined to body, mind, sense, none but He enjoys.[2]

The analogy is exact, whether it be for the individual body or the body of the State. The two reflect each other. Thus, we all have within us a monarch and a government capable of responding to the rule of reason—'sovereign reason', as Shakespeare calls it. The trouble begins when we begin to doubt ourselves and lose self-respect. That self-respect as a nation or as an individual is all-important. Without it we lose sovereignty, which is the ability to rule ourselves—or, more accurately, the Self ruling us.

> He who calls intellect to manage the reins of his mind reaches the end of his journey, finds there all-pervading Spirit.[3]

The importance of having a monarch is thus demonstrated as a visible symbol of unity with the One Self in the affairs of the State. This sense of unity at national level is vital to the State, as it is at all levels: the family, the nation, all humanity. Perhaps most important is the sense of unity of the individual. As wise Plato observed, the individual and the state reflect each other. In *The Republic* Socrates has a conversation with Adeimantus:

> ... suppose that a short-sighted person had been asked by someone to read small letters from a distance; and it occurred to someone else that they might be found in another place which was larger and in which the letters were larger—if they were the same and he could read the larger letters first, and then proceed to the lesser—this would have been thought a rare piece of good fortune.

Very true, said Adeimantus; but how does the illustration apply to our enquiry?

I will tell you, I replied; justice, which is the subject of our enquiry, is, as you know, sometimes spoken of as the virtue of an individual, and sometimes as the virtue of a State.

True, he replied.

And is not the State larger than an individual?

It is.

Then in the larger the quantity of justice is likely to be larger and more easily discernible. I propose therefore that we enquire into the nature of justice and injustice, first as they appear in the State, and secondly in the individual, proceeding from the greater to the lesser and comparing them.[4]

But we can deprecate the monarchy, lose faith in it, ignore it or treat it with contempt, in the same way as we mock ourselves and the divinity within each of us. The two attitudes are related: inasmuch as we mock monarchy so we mock ourselves and are belittled by it. What is needed is a triumphant assertion of the values to be found in the Crown and that we will find abundantly in the hearts and voices of the people, this Jubilee Year.

The mass of people understand this but the chattering classes do not. Our great constitutional scholar, Walter Bagehot, wrote:

The best reason why monarchy is a strong government is, that it is an intelligible government. The mass of mankind understand it, and they hardly anywhere in the world understand any other . . . .. When you put before the mass of mankind the question, 'Will you be governed by a king, or will you be governed by a constititution?' the inquiry comes out thus: 'Will you be governed in a way you understand, or will you be governed in a way you do not understand?'[5]

I venture to suggest this is still true today, despite our apparently more sophisticated society. The alternative is to be governed by an

increasing number of dictators. The world is now full of supposed
'democracies' ruled by strong men, imposing their authority on
threatened and bewildered populations. We have a recent example
in Zimbabwe where the head of state is a ruthless and corrupt
dictator and the people suffer. As one voter said, 'He will take us
down with him'. And yet, you know, wise Plato tells us we always
get the government we deserve.

The twenty-five or so monarchies are the most stable societies,
even though some of them rank among the autocracies.

The need of humanity to reach out and touch eternity is exemp-
lified in the United States and the treatment there of its presidents.
Michael Novak wrote about the kind of monarchical reverence
which the President attracts:

> Hands are stretched toward him over wire fences at airports like
> hands extended toward medieval sovereigns or ancient prophets.
> One wonders what mystic participation our presidents convey,
> what witness from what other world, what form of cure or
> heightened life. The president arouses waves of 'power', 'being',
> 'superior reality', as if where he is is history . . ... His office is, in
> quite modern and sophisticated form, a religion in a secular
> state. It evokes responses familiar in all the ancient religions of
> the world. It fills a perennial vacuum at the heart of human
> expectations.[6]

But if the heart of human expectations meets the crudity and corruption of such presidents as Richard Nixon then there is a trau-
matic effect across the nation. People lose faith in the presidential
system. They no longer trust their leaders. There is cynicism about
politics and presidents. Less than half the electorate bothers to vote
and, when it does, as shown by the recent national poll, the result is
indecisive. Did Bush win or did Gore amass enough punched cards
in the State of Florida? Worse are the long-serving and highly
corrupt presidencies of men like Mitterand in France, with their
hands thrust into the public purse and ambition geared to further
electoral success.

Far better, surely, to have as head of state a monarch who can have no further public ambition; whose training in early life is towards service to all; whose means are sufficient not to make money a goal; who can restrain the corruption of prime ministers, as George V did with Lloyd George; and above all, a monarch who has the time and freedom to stand back from the political fray for the long-term benefit of the nation.

It is a very great asset, this freedom for the head of state to stand back, like the passenger in the chariot, constantly attentive to what is going on in government, but not intervening unless in an emergency. That The Queen does have a residual power to intervene, should the democratic basis of the constitution be threatened, is accepted by the leading writers on the constitution.[7] The principle is, 'The Queen can do no wrong'. The corollary to that is she can only do right. That is to say, whatever is right or true for the people. This is the law which governs the Crown and which is found in the coronation service, about which I have written a book entitled *The Royal Law*, and which is expressed in the judicial oath sworn by all her judges:

> ... I will do right to all manner of people after the laws and usages of this realm, without fear or favour, affection or ill-will. So help me God.

It was amply demonstrated in 1975 when her Governor-General of Australia was forced to dismiss a prime minister and government which had grossly abused their powers. The country was polarised and paralysed. Sir John Kerr consulted the Australian Chief Justice and then acted to free the democratic process to call new elections. There was nothing unconstitutional in that. The prerogative powers of the Crown—powers to act in an emergency—are part of the Common Law and therefore subject to review by the Courts.

It is when prime ministers are overwhelmed by the very events that they claim they can control that the monarchy operates to stiffen their backbones. Prime ministers can panic at the awful vista of consequences looming from decisions taken, and they seek solace from the Palace. This happened with the banking crisis of 1931 when MacDonald was on the point of resigning as Prime Minister. Instead, the King, George V, summoned a conference at Buckingham Palace, attended by the three leaders of the political parties, MacDonald, Baldwin and Samuel. According to the note made by the King's Private Secretary, 'The King assured the Prime Minister that, remaining at his post, his position and reputation would be much more enhanced than if he surrendered the government of the country at such a crisis. Baldwin and Samuel said they were willing to serve under the Prime Minister, and render all help possible to carry on the Government as a National Emergency Government until an emergency bill or bills had been passed by Parliament, which would restore once more British credit and the confidence of foreigners. After that they would expect His Majesty to grant a dissolution. To this course the King agreed . . ..' It is certainly not unthinkable that the same might happen again, given the very wide range of problems being heaped on the head of a modern prime minister. He or she could expect the same re-assurance, wisdom and direction and a practical approach to the crisis.

The founding sentence of our Common Law constitution, written by a judge, Henry de Bracton in the thirteenth century, is: 'The King must not be under man but under God and the law, because law makes the King'.[8] The entire passage in which he makes this statement, for its language and its reason, is worth quoting:

> The king must not be under man but under God and under the law, because law makes the king. Let him therefore bestow upon the law what the law bestows upon him, namely rule and power, for there is no 'rex' where will rules rather than 'lex'. Since he is the vicar of God there ought to be no one in his kingdom who surpasses him in the doing of justice. And that he ought to be under the law appears clearly in the analogy of Jesus Christ, whose viceregent on earth he is, for though many ways were open to [Christ] for his ineffable redemption of the human race,

the true mercy of God chose this most powerful way to destroy the devil's work, he would not use the power of force but the reason of justice. Thus [Christ] willed himself to be under law that He might redeem those who live under it.

What a contrast between this sense of freedom and rightness and the ruling precept on the Continent of Europe—which still prevails—and which was commented on by another judge, Sir John Fortescue, in the fifteenth century. He called his great work In Praise of the Laws of England which gave me the idea for the title of this lecture. Fortescue was a Chief Justice under Henry VI and shared his exile in France. There he wrote this prescient passage:

The King of England is not able to change the laws of his kingdom at pleasure, for he rules his people with a government not only regal but also political. If he were to preside over them with a power entirely regal, he would be able to change the laws of his realm, and also to impose on them [taxes] and other burdens without consulting them. This is the sort of dominion which the Civil Laws indicate when they state 'What has pleased the prince has the force of law'. But the case is far otherwise with the king who rules his people politically, because he is not able himself to change the laws without the assent of his subjects, nor to burden an unwilling people with strange imposts . . ..[9]

'What has pleased the prince has the force of law'. Still this maxim of Justinian is the basis of government in continental Europe. Imagine the loss of freedom if we surrender the Common Law of England which, through devices such as habeas corpus, preserves individual liberty, and through judicial review restrains government from adopting powers not given by statute or by law. Note that in countries like France almost the reverse is true: the government official has wide, amorphous powers and the individual gets only those rights which are granted by the State and which may be taken away from him.

But if the monarchy stands apart from the everyday politics of the State it is certainly not the case that it does not care for the future of the nation. Indeed, that is a prime function of monarchy, just as the charioteer steers the chariot in a path free of perils. Where The Queen necessarily must move privately The Prince of Wales can speak boldly and can challenge the goals towards which current policies are taking us. In this His Royal Highness is following in the footsteps of his forebear, Prince Albert, The Prince Consort, who overcame resistance to new ideas, new technology, new scientific discoveries.

The Prince of Wales works subtly, with wit and wisdom, in reminding us of the values we should cherish and maintain for the future happiness of our children and grandchildren. About Shakespeare he said on one occasion:

> Many 'ordinary' parents, I suspect, would agree that education is not about social engineering, but about preparing our children as best we can for all the challenges in front of them. This means not only training them for work through the acquisition of knowledge, but also giving them an understanding of themselves and of the deeper meaning of life . . ..
>
> Shakespeare holds up a mirror for us to see ourselves and to experience ourselves, so that we gain in the process a more profound understanding of ourselves and others, appreciating right and wrong, and the factors which make us behave as we do . . ..
>
> Despite all the dramatic changes that have been wrought by science and technology, and the remarkable benefits they have brought us, there remains deep in the soul of each of us, I believe, a vital metaphysical ingredient which makes life worth living. This awareness of a spiritual dimension greater than, and beyond, the confines of our everyday self, and of a purely superficial perception of the physical world in which we exist, has a particular link to aesthetic experience, and to literature . . ..
>
> I don't want my children—or anybody else's—to be deprived of Shakespeare, or of the other life-enhancing elements which I

have suggested should be part of the schooling entitlement of all the children of the country . . .. But I fear that these are real dangers if we evade those key questions about the nature and purpose of education which I have touched on today, and if we fail to give our schools and our teachers the resources, and the philosophical framework, they need to produce the right results.[10]

To the Royal College of Psychiatrists he said:

I do not expect you to agree with me, but I believe that the most urgent need for western man is to rediscover that divine element in his being, without which there can never be any possible hope or meaning to our existence in the earthly realm.[11]

Just two examples from many of the forward-looking Prince, concerned with the future health of his kingdom. But he is also concerned with the here and now, in terms of employment and opportunity. Through The Prince's Trust and other charitable concerns The Prince has generated new businesses and jobs for thousands of young people. James Morton, who wrote about these endeavours in a book entitled *Breaking the Cycle*,[12] said:

His work has brought tangible improvements to the lives of over 600,000 disadvantaged young people and in the process generated benefits for the country with a value approaching £12 billion . . .. The institution of monarchy provides [The Prince's] family with an opportunity to think within a timescale which may seem irrelevant to everyday life but could matter a great deal to our grandchildren. He has a vision for the country he would like Britain to be today and also far into the future.

But we make a huge mistake if we think that the political side of the Crown is the most important. It is not. As a *Times* editorial said: 'The Crown rests at the apex of civil society, what the historian

Frank Prochaska has called the "commonwealth of citizenship out-side the State".[13] That is to say, The Queen is head of all civil society, not just the innovating bit represented by politicians who come and go with the tides of time. They may think they are supreme, outdoing The Queen, but politicians are ruled by the ideas of a previous generation or, as Maynard Keynes so famously put it, 'they are usually the slaves of some defunct economist'.[14] The current Prime Minister is the tenth of the present Queen's advisers.

The Queen is effectively head of the permanent institutions by which the country is actually ruled and which lend their power to the government of the moment—institutions such as the Church, the Law Courts, the Universities, the Civil Service and the Armed Forces. In another editorial The Times said:

> The sovereign state of Britain is the Crown in Parliament. The system of parliamentary democracy embraces the notion of governments formed from parliamentary majorities for limited periods of office, with regular provision for peaceful change when the parliamentary majority reflects a different balance of political interest. To be loyal to the principles of parliamentary democracy involves a residual disloyalty to the government of the day since it must imply acceptance that a different government with dif-ferent policies from the present one would also command the same loyalty from its servants and the other state institutions as this one does.... Ministers may have their parliamentary majority behind them and it may give them temporary power to use the permanent institutions of the state to further their policies. But those institutions will outlast them and be at the service of their political opponents.[15]

The natural place for these institutions to meet and examine the legislative plans of any government is the House of Lords. But there is little or no appreciation of the purpose and function of the Lords. I grant that hereditary peers should not, in a democratic age, dominate the House: but they should be represented there, as they are directly derived from, and support, the Crown, which is also a hereditary office. Our great jurist of the eighteenth century Sir William Blackstone wrote:

> And herein indeed consists the true excellence of the English government, that all parts of it form a mutual check upon each other. In the legislature, the people are a check upon the nobility, and the nobility a check upon the people.[16]

It has nothing to do with class division, but everything to do with checks and balances. At the time of the restoration of the monarchy, in 1660, Parliament declared that 'according to the *ancient and fundamental laws* of this kingdom the government is and ought to be by King, Lords and Commons'.[17] This would appear to entrench a constitutional principle which an ordinary Act of Parliament could not reach. The concept of the Crown embraces all our social activities and The Queen is watchful over all of them. This is known as 'The Queen's Peace'. Frank Prochaska, in his book *Royal Bounty*,[18] addresses one aspect of this Peace:

> Britain's philanthropic traditions, so instrumental in civil life and liberty, are profound. The Crown's contribution to these traditions has been and continues to be enabling. The abolition of the monarchy, whatever the benefits, would mark another stage in the perfection of the state monolith. Moreover, it would eliminate that part of the constitution that serves as a buffer between the state and society . . .. The first lady [of the United States], however many of her charities, cannot be compared to the Queen as a focus of civil society.

We are dependent on that Queen's Peace. Notice how she goes about it: she moves serenely, and with the majesty which is my topic today. Her Peace holds us in place and serves to remind us of ourselves. Without that peace we should be as agitated and unquiet as unchecked horses, the senses, pulling the chariot of the State. Fortunately there is another, very practical, answer to those who would do away with the monarchy: The Queen is not only sovereign of the United Kingdom, but also she is Head of the Common-wealth, and Queen of the kingdoms therein represented—Canada, Australia, New Zealand. Dispensing with the monarchy if it were ever tried, would entail obtaining the consent of these other king-doms, and the other, smaller overseas dependencies. The revo-lutionaries campaigned long and hard, but Australia voted recently to retain the monarchy.

There is, however, another way of attacking monarchy, which is being tried. This is to denigrate the institution, in all sorts of subtle ways. For example, the royal writ has gone from the Courts, by which litigating parties were summoned to a third point, The Queen's Judges, to determine their quarrels and restore The Queen's Peace. Jurors used to swear an oath that they would well and truly try the several issues joined between our Sovereign Lady The Queen and the defendant and a true verdict give according to the evidence. Now, because it is thought this was too much of a mouthful for the ordinary juror (how patronising we have become!) he or she merely swears to well and truly try the *defendant*. Did no one ever bother to explain to a deaf Lord Chancellor the difference between trying *the issues* and trying *the defendant*?

If monarchy is denigrated so are our country and ourselves. There is a demonic purpose in all this: the more self-respect we lose the greater slavery can be imposed upon us. Not for nothing does the title European Convention on Human Rights include the words *and Freedoms*. Note the plural. Freedom is absolute, freedom cannot be divided into sections which are accorded to you by a gracious State, and taken away if you misbehave. President Kennedy once observed: 'Freedom is indivisible, and when one man is enslaved, all are not free'.

Royalty is an act of imagination. A republic is a thing of intellect only. Bagehot wrote:

> It is often said that men are ruled by their imaginations; but it would be truer to say they are governed by the weakness of their imaginations.

I had the privilege recently of talking to a class of young girls about the monarchy. We showed them a video of the coronation. They were fascinated by the colour and the pageantry. No need to instruct them in the dry text of the constitution. They got the point of it at once, through the heart. And they asked all the most important questions, such as, 'What is the coach made of?' And, 'Does The Queen have cousins?' Even at the age of eight or nine it can be appreciated that The Queen has authority and power. She exercises authority through subtle influence, akin to what Disraeli described in a speech at Manchester in 1872:

> I know it will be said that ... the personal influence of the Sovereign is now merged in the responsibility of the Minister. I think you will find a great fallacy in this view. The principles of the English Constitution do not contemplate the absence of personal influence on the part of the Sovereign; and, if they did, the principles of human nature would prevent the fulfilment of such a theory.

Or, in the words of Bagehot:

> To state the matter shortly, the sovereign has, under a constitutional monarchy such as ours, three rights—the right to be consulted, the right to encourage, the right to warn. And a king of great sense and sagacity would want no others. He would find that his having no others would enable him to use these with singular effect. He would say to his minister: 'The responsibility of these measures is upon you. Whatever you think best must be done. Whatever you think best shall have my full and effectual support. But you will observe for this reason and that reason what you propose to do is bad; for this reason and that reason what you do not propose is better. I do not oppose, it is my duty not to oppose; but observe that I *warn*.' Supposing the king to be right, and to have what kings often have, the gift of effectual expression he could not help moving his minister.

He might not always turn his course, but he would always trouble his mind.[19]

The point is, all this is done privately. We used to go to great lengths to preserve the unitary character of our constitution, so that, for example, the high office of Lord Chancellor, under The Queen, had judicial, legislative and executive roles to play. Now the divisive nature of the Human Rights Act will probably see those functions scattered. If one wants evidence of the lack of thought which now predominates in our so-called constitutional innovation, one has only to look at the position of The Queen under the Scotland Act 1998, granting devolution to Scotland. The Scottish Parliament is unicameral, which means there is no independent check on the whims and fancies of the democratic assembly. The Queen must agree to Scottish legislation, on the advice of the First Minister in Scotland. But no one has anticipated what might happen if she is advised one way by the First Minister in Scotland, but in another way by the Prime Minister of the United Kingdom.

What is to be made of media outbursts against the supposed costs of the monarchy, to the extent of The Queen paying income tax, when it should be widely known that the annual income from the Crown Estates, which goes directly to the Treasury, amounted in 2000–1 to £133 million and the cost to the Treasury of the monarchy, including the upkeep of palaces, was £35 million. So, we make a profit from the monarchy![20]

These are all material considerations. Far more important to our well-being is the spiritual dimension of the monarchy. This spiritual dimension is the subject of a recently published book, by the Reverend Dr Ian Bradley, entitled God Save the Queen. In it Dr Bradley reprints a letter of his published in The Times in November 1977, part of which is as follows:

In all this talk of a Royal Family more in touch with public opinion, we are in danger of missing the essential nature and purpose of monarchy. The monarchy is not a democratic institution, still less the creature of public opinion, but rather a divinely instituted symbol and mystery. At their coronations, our kings and queens are anointed in a ritual which has its origins in Old Testament times and underlines the spiritual nature of their calling. They are thereafter accountable first and foremost to God and not to a fickle populace so easily manipulated and swayed by the mass media. Their role may not be to lead public opinion, though in deep and subtle ways they can both express the mood of the nation and also exert a powerful example, but most certainly they are not there to pander to it.

We need to think much more about the religious basis of monarchy and the exercise of its spiritual function. In the case of our present Queen, it has been expressed in a sacrificial commitment to duty and public service and a sure and steadfast Christian faith fortified and nourished through regular churchgoing. In the case of her eldest son, who I fervently hope will be our next King, it may well take a different form, in keeping with his declared desire to be a defender of faith and his deep sensitivity to spiritual issues.[21]

At the very end of his book, Dr. Bradley says:

Ultimately, monarchy points beyond itself to the majesty of God. It encourages the God-given human faculties of reverence, loyalty and worship. This is the real sacramentality of monarchy. It derives its true sanction from above rather than from below . . .. What our sovereign needs and deserves most of all from us is our loyal and heartfelt prayer. O Lord, save the Queen, and mercifully hear us when we call upon Thee![22]

The Queen is one of the few current Heads of State to be consecrated to the task. In the ceremony of coronation she gives her oath, which is sacred, and which no minister should cause her to disobey. The oath, which is embodied in the Coronation Oath Act of 1689, was administered by the Archbishop at the coronation in 1953 as follows:

40

Archbishop   Will you solemnly promise and swear to govern the Peoples of the United Kingdom of Great Britain and Northern Ireland, Canada, Australia, New Zealand, the Union of South Africa, Pakistan and Ceylon, and of your Possessions and the other Territories to any of them belonging or pertaining, according to their respective laws and customs?

The Queen   I solemnly promise so to do.

Archbishop   Will you to your power cause Law and Justice, in Mercy, to be executed in all your judgments?

The Queen   I will.

Archbishop   Will you to the utmost of your power maintain the Laws of God and the true profession of the Gospel? Will you to the utmost of your power maintain in the United Kingdom the Protestant Reformed Religion established by law? Will you maintain and preserve inviolably the settlement of the Church of England, and the doctrine, worship, discipline and government thereof, as by law established in England? And will you preserve unto the Bishops and Clergy of England, and to the Churches there committed to their charge, all such rights and privileges, as by law do or shall appertain to them or any of them?

The Queen   All this I promise to do.

No doubt at the next coronation there will be much scratching of heads over the formal religious part of the oath, especially regarding the Church of England. But all this oath does is remind us of the primacy of the Christian religion in the maintenance of this State, no matter how many other faiths are represented at the ceremony; and to recognise the necessity for the Church to be an active part of government. In this respect one is reminded of the words of Archbishop Wulfstan in Anglo-Saxon times:

> . . . true it is what I say, if Christianity be weakened, the kingdom will forthwith totter; and if bad laws be set up anywhere in the nation, or vicious habits be anywhere too much loved, that will

be all to the nation's detriment; but let be done as it is requisite, let unrighteousness be suppressed, and God's righteousness upraised; that may be beneficial before God, and before the world. Amen.

At a later stage of the coronation, the Archbishop uses these words:

... With this Sword do justice, stop the growth of iniquity, protect the holy Church of God, help and defend widows and orphans, restore the things that are gone to decay, maintain the things that are restored, punish and reform what is amiss, and confirm what is in good order . . ..

Our present Queen takes this oath most seriously. The magnificent words of the coronation service are a song of praise at the heart of our constitution. Not many countries praise God in quite this way when installing a new Head of State. The present situation of the monarchy is perhaps best set out in an ancient, Vedic story about kingship:

There was a king who was visited by a holy man. After giving him his respects, the king asked for his blessing and advice. As a king, he wanted to be good and just, so he looked for some good advice.

The holy man said that if he could do just one thing he would do well in every walk of life, and that thing is the Truth. Stay with the Truth, leave everything else. Other things will take care of themselves.

The king noted the advice and resolved to put it into practice. Soon he was known as a man of Truth. One of the rules in his kingdom was that the state used to buy all of the goods in the evening which could not be sold in the market and use them as need arose. This was to ensure no working man was disappointed by not selling his produce.

A clever man, having known that the king would stand by his

word, tried to test the king and at the same time gain something out of it. He collected all the rubbish he could find, put it in a box and went to the market to sell it. No one would buy the rubbish and he was left with all he had brought. In the evening the officers arrived and noted the situation. They said that this was rubbish and no commodity, but as the rule stands, we will pay your expenses for having come to this place and you may dump the rubbish somewhere else. The clever man said that he would either sell it or take it home for 'I will not be in a hurry to dispose of my valuable goods'. The officers understood that he was not joking but bent upon testing the strength of the king's rule. He was asked what price he expected and demanded a hundred thousand rupees. The officers were astonished and took him to the king. Finally the king had to pay. The rubbish was dumped in the palace.

During the night, the king found the goddess Lakshmi (goddess of wealth) in front of him, saying 'Your palace is full of rubbish. I do not want to stay in such a filthy place, so I am leaving your kingdom'. The king was sorry, but he let her go. After Lakshmi all gods and goddesses left the kingdom, one after the other, for there was no Lakshmi. Art, wisdom, crafts, honour and sundry others all walked away. Finally the king was faced by Narayana (the Absolute) and He said: 'There is no good company here in your kingdom. My wife, Lakshmi, and all the others have left you, so I must leave too'. The king said, 'No. You cannot. You have no reason to leave me for You are the Truth and I am still holding to the Truth. Only if you find me engaged in untruth may You go'. The king was right so Narayana had to stay. After some time Lakshmi returned, saying 'How can I live without my husband? So here I am'. Others came following her and the kingdom was restored to its power and glory once again.[23]

In a way, our Queen is in a similar situation. The country is full of rubbish in the arts and generally. The gods are not in our favour. Materiality abounds, and selfishness and violence. Yet The Queen stands by the Truth. She speaks Truth. There may be hope for the return of well-being and prosperity.

May I remind you of the second verse of our National Anthem:

> *The choicest gifts in store*
> *On her be pleased to pour;*
> *Long may she reign!*
> *May she defend our laws,*
> *And ever give us cause*
> *To sing with heart and voice*
> *God save the Queen*

If God saves the Queen there is a chance for the rest of us!

NOTES

1. Nicolson, *King George V* (Constable, 1952), 146-7.

2. Ed. Shree Purohit Swami, *The Ten Principal Upanishads* (Faber, 1937), 32.

3. Ibid. 32.

4. *The Republic* 368.

5. *The Collected Works of Bagehot*, V.226.

6. Quoted in Cronin, *The State of the Presidency* (Little, Brown, 1975), 87.

7. See Jennings, *Cabinet Government* (Cambridge, 1969); R. Brazier, *The Nature of the Crown* (Oxford), 343; V. Bogdanor, *The Monarchy & Constitution* (Oxford), 77–8.

8. Ed. Woodbine, *On the Laws & Customs of England* (Harvard, 1968), II.33.

9. Quoted in L. L. Blake, *Sovereignty: Power Beyond Politics* (Shepheard-Walwyn, 1988), 45.

10. *Annual Shakespeare Birthday Lecture*, 1991.

11. 5 July 1991.

12. Ebury Press, 1998.

13. 26 October 1996.

14. *The General Theory* Book VI, ch. 24.

15. 25 February 1985.

16. *Commentaries* Book 1, ch. 2.

17. J. R. Tanner, *English Constitutional Conflicts of the 17th Century* (Cambridge, 1928), 290.

18. Page 282.

19. *The English Constitution* (Third Edition, 1882), 75.

20. See Simon Heffer, *The Spectator* 2 March 2002.

21. Ian Bradley, *God Save The Queen* (Darton, Longman & Todd, 2002), xv.

22. Ibid. 204.

23. I am indebted to S. M. Jaiswal for the translation of this story.

JOHN CAREY

IDEAL KINGSHIP IN EARLY IRELAND

There have not always been kings in Ireland. In the canonical account of Ireland's legendary history, as this is set forth in the eleventh-century treatise known as the Book of Taking, no kings are associated with the first three settlements of the island, those of the followers of Cesair, of Partholón, and of Nemed.[1] Kingship came first with the Fir Bolg—an ancient tribe whose name points to their kinship with the Belgae of Britain and the Continent, who were described by Caesar as the most traditional, and consequently the most bellicose, of the peoples whom he encountered during his campaigns in Gaul.[2] The Fir Bolg kings of Ireland were for their own part warlike enough: out of seven successions to the throne, four involved the incumbent's death in battle. No such internecine violence is said to have characterised the earlier inhabitants of Ireland.

But although the tradition depicts kingship in Ireland as having been, from its beginnings, inseparable from bloodshed, another element is at least as important: the creation of an enduring framework for society. The Fir Bolg were the first to occupy the site of Tara, symbol ever since of the dream of national unity; and it is they who divided Ireland into five provinces—a paradigmatic geography which, on the analogy of similar demarcations in Iceland, China and elsewhere, can be understood as assimilating the island to the cosmos as a whole.[3] Echu son of Erc, the last of the Fir Bolg kings, is described as having presided over a short-lived Golden Age:

> Echu son of Erc ruled for ten years. There was no rain, but only dew during that time; there was no year without acorns. Spears [or lies] were banished from Ireland in his time. It is by him that law was first enacted in Ireland.

But Echu too was slain, and a poem laments his passing. This poem opens as follows:

> Answer my questions, lad,
> and tell me tales:
> it is long since every evil was spread abroad
> after the body of Echu son of Erc was pierced.
>
> Echu son of Erc: such was his virtue
> that he was better than any king except holy Christ.
> He is the first king who was wounded
> with a spear in white Ireland . . ..
>
> There was no peace nor ease in it—
> a frenzy of grief was on the multitude—
> from peaceful noble Echu
> until the time of great Míl's sons [i.e., the first Gaels].

At the conclusion, the poet implicitly likens this long-ago calamity to a more recent murder:

> There is done in enduring Breffny
> a deed which will cause much sorrow—
> the oak-land is sorrowful once more—
> the killing of the pilgrim from Rome.
>
> Nertach son of Domnall wreaks
> the holy one's destruction—may his house-post be crooked!
> There will not be in Ireland, without blame,
> woman nor farm nor fire nor smoke.[4]

This vivid evocation of the Waste Land is also a description, presumably, of the affliction which Ireland endured after Echu's death.

The figure of Echu son of Erc, remembered as having been the first of Ireland's ideal kings, illustrates themes which are of importance to the ideology of Irish kingship as a whole. One of these is the belief that a realm justly ruled will enjoy not merely social well-being but also the blessings of nature: clement weather and abundant harvests. The other is the comparison, expressed in the poem by the statement that Echu was better than any king save Christ, between the just king and the Christian God.

Both themes appear again in a brief tract which is probably the oldest Irish treatise on kingship that has come down to us. This document comprises one section of a Latin work, evidently composed in the seventh century, whose title can be translated as *The Twelve Misuses of this World*. These 'misuses' are persons who lack the virtues which should be their primary characteristics: an irreligious old man, a disobedient youth, an ungenerous rich man, a woman without modesty, and so on. The ninth is the *rex iniquus* or 'unjust king', of whom we are told that

since he ought to be the corrector of the unjust, he does not preserve in himself even the dignity of his name. For the name of 'king' (*rex*) preserves the idea that he ought to exercise the office of guide (*rector*) to those who are his subjects. But how can he correct others, when he does not correct his own behaviour, lest it be unjust? For the throne is exalted in the king's justice, and the government of the peoples is made firm in truth . . ..

Whoever does not administer the realm according to this law, will suffer very many misfortunes in his reign. For on that account the peace of the peoples is often shattered, and even scandals concerning the realm are stirred up; moreover the fruits of the earth diminish, and the service of the people is thwarted; many and varied sorrows afflict the prosperity of the realm; the deaths of loved ones and of children bring grief; enemy raids lay territories waste on every side; beasts ravage the flocks of sheep and cattle; tempests of the air, and troubled skies, blight the fruitfulness of the earth and the bounty of the sea; and from time to time strokes of lightning burn up the fields, the blossoms of the trees, and the leaves of vines.

The king's justice, on the other hand,

> is the peace of peoples, the guarding of the land, the protection
> of the populace, the defence of the race, the cure of weaknesses,
> the joy of men, clemency of the air, calm of the sea, fruitfulness of
> the earth, the comfort of the poor, an inheritance for his sons,
> and for himself the hope of future blessedness.[5]

The idea that misrule brings cosmic as well as social evils, while
a harmonious reign is reflected in the harmony of nature, could
hardly be expressed more plainly. The analogy between divine and
human kingship is also present here, but more subtly so. The statement 'the throne is exalted in the king's justice, and the government of the peoples is made firm in truth' alludes to two passages in
the Bible: Psalm 88:17 ('they will be exalted in Your justice') and
Proverbs 16:12 ('the throne is made firm in justice'). In the first of
these, it is God's justice which is meant rather than that of any
earthly king: for the Irish text, then, it seems to be implied that the
justice essential to rightful rule on earth is also ultimately divine.

If the king resembles God, then God is imagined as a king.
Indeed, early Irish writers dwell insistently on God's royalty: again
and again he is called Rí ('King');[6] the word for the highest heaven,
ríched, is an archaic compound which originally meant 'the King's
seat';[7] and the term 'high king' seems to have been applied to God
long before it came to be associated with the lordship of Tara.[8] The
eighth-century poet Blathmac, as he imagined himself joining
Mary in her keening for her crucified Son, thought of Christ as a
monarch to whom the Jews owed obedience both as kinsmen and as
vassals. He expresses his indignation in language which bristles
with traditional legal terminology:

> Shameless their faces, wolflike the men
> who wrought that kin-slaying.
> Since his mother was one of them,
> it was utter betrayal of a near kinsman.

The son of God the Father, moreover,
Christ, our royally generous Over-king,
had often given them [gifts], after that,
[in answer] to many remarkable requests . . ..

Every fine thing which the King granted
to the Jews, in exchange for their service,
was 'wealth to slaves':
they have spoiled what was allotted them . . ..

Bad were the valuations of [Judas]:
it was a false judgment, his estimation.
Even a strong enduring board of red gold
were a poor price for Christ, son of God . . ..

A grief to me is Christ on the cross—
greater his suffering than every noble doomed one—
because of how well he distributed wealth,
silver and lovely wares.[9]

Similar ideas can be traced in one of the earliest surviving Irish poems, dating apparently from a time when the conversion to Christianity was still a thing of the relatively recent past. A eulogy of the legendary dynast Labraid the Exile, nicknamed Moen or 'the Silent One', compares his lordship over men to the Christian God's supremacy over the divinities of the pagans:

The grandson of Loegaire Lorc
was a gryphon attacking unknown lands:
loftier than men
save for the Heaven-King of heaven.

Gold [brighter] than the great shining sun,
he conquered the worlds of men.
Moen son of the sole king Áine
is [like] the One God compared with the gods.[10]

It may be felt that there is nothing especially surprising in any of this. The divinisation of kings is probably as old and as widespread as kingship itself; and, within a Christian context, the paradoxical image of the 'kingdom of heaven' is one of the main themes of the Gospels. Why should such analogies be assigned any particular importance when they appear in Irish sources?

To this reasonable question there are at least two answers. For one thing, the mere fact of a phenomenon's being widely attested does not mean that it may not be worth while to study its individual manifestations. But in the present case we need not stop at generalities. The image of God as king *does* seem to have received a special emphasis in medieval Ireland, and to have been explored in distinctive ways. What these were will become clearer if we consider a few more pieces of evidence in the early literature.

In a recent essay, I have attempted to sketch some of the ideas lying behind the remarkable theological treatise *On the Miracles of Holy Scripture*, written in Ireland in the middle of the seventh century.[11] Central to the author's conception of the miraculous was the doctrine that God's relationship with the universe underwent a radical change following the sixth day of creation. In his own words,

> We both believe that He finished all things on the sixth day and rested on the seventh, and also do not doubt that He is working until now. But we must consider more carefully how the same God can be considered to have finished then, and to be working now.
>
> On the sixth day He completed his work on the natures of created things, but even now He does not cease to govern them; and on the seventh day He rested from the work of creation, but He never ceases from the exercise of government. For we are to understand that God was a Creator then, but is a Governor now. Therefore if among created things we see anything new arise, God should not be thought to have created a new nature, but to be governing that which He created formerly.[12]

How all of this relates to the understanding of miracles does not, of course, bear directly on the present subject. What is relevant, however, is the conviction that God's sovereignty over His creation is conditioned, at the most fundamental level, by an obligation to sustain the cosmic harmony which He established in the beginning. If the Divine King is characterised as preserving the natural order, it seems fitting that that order should also be promoted, on the human plane, by the exercise of righteous kingship.

For Celticists, the classic description of the cosmic benefits of royal justice is that which is given in *The Testament of Morand*: this is the oldest treatise on kingship in the Irish language, probably composed a generation later than *On the Miracles of Holy Scripture*.[13] The passage in question runs as follows:

> It is through the truth of the ruler that plagues, a great army, or lightnings are averted from people. It is through the truth of the ruler that he judges great kingdoms, great riches. It is through the truth of the ruler that he consummates peace, ease, joy, repose, comfort. It is through the truth of the ruler that he drives back great armies as far as the borders of their allies. It is through the truth of the ruler that every heir establishes himself in his fair inheritance. It is through the truth of the ruler that the manna of the great acorn-yield of a great wood is tasted. It is through the truth of the ruler that the milk of a great herd of cattle is enriched. It is through the truth of the ruler that there is every abundance of high, lofty grain. It is through the truth of the ruler that greatness of fish swims in the streams. It is through the truth of the ruler that fair offspring are well begotten.[14]

The king's truth and the order of the cosmos appear here as correlative, almost as aspects of one another. Again, this is an ancient and widespread idea: Homer and Hesiod speak in similar terms of δίκη or 'justice';[15] while it is said in the Rig Veda that 'the rivers pour forth justice (ṛta), the sun has spread out truth (satya)'.[16]

That the mortal king, like God, has the duty of upholding the order of creation is also expressed in another way in *The Testament of Morand*: it is the king who assigns their proper values to all of the things which exist within his realm. Morand, the dying sage, includes the following among the instructions which his disciple is to convey to the new king Feradach:

> Say to him that he should assess the creatures of the Creator, He Who has created them as they have been created. Every precious thing which he will not judge according to its gifts, it will not yield them with full fruit. Let him assess the earth according to its fruits. Let him assess the yew according to its wares. Let him assess cattle according to their illustrious visitation. Let him assess milk according to its increases. Let him assess grain according to its height. Let him assess streams by their full washing.

And so on: the king is to determine the worth of iron, bronze, silver and gold; of the soil; of sheep and pigs; of warriors and underlings; of old men; of fathers and mothers; of the work of craftsmen.

> Let him assess what is correct and proper, truth and order, the contract and settlement of every prince of truth to all his subjects. Let him assess the proper worth of every rank, of the noble classes and of the non-noble classes.[17]

More is involved here than the simple notion of nature's bounty being a reward for virtuous rule. God's creatures actually depend upon the utterance of the king's judgments in order to realise the whole of their potential. Earthly kingship does not merely mimic divine kingship, therefore: it actually completes the work of the Creator.

It is probably no coincidence that this cluster of associations can be paralleled in some of what the Bible has to tell us concerning the first of earthly rulers, who is also the prototype and forebear of all humanity. Not only was Adam made 'in the image and likeness' of God, and instructed to 'subjugate and rule over' all living creatures, but he was entrusted with the special task of naming the beasts:

> [God] brought them to Adam, so that He might see what he would call them; for whatever Adam called a living thing, that is its name.[18]

Here we have something closely comparable to the 'assessing' of all creatures which Morand enjoins on Feradach: to name a thing, and to establish its value, are two ways of seeking to articulate its essential being.

*

The ideas found in these texts are couched in Christian terms; but their roots must reach back, in part at least, to times before the coming of Christianity. Thus the Roman historian Livy speaks of a Celtic king named Ambigatus, the virtue of whose rule was apparent from the circumstance that 'in his reign Gaul was so fruitful in crops and in men that it scarcely seemed possible to rule over the abounding multitude'.[19]

An Irish story, which surely also reflects an earlier myth, describes the adventures of Íth, the first of the Gaels to come to Ireland. At that time the country was inhabited by the Tuatha Dé, the 'Tribes of the Gods', whose three kings were married to three goddesses whose names were the names of Ireland. After a long journey, Íth came to where the kings were seeking to divide the property of a lord who had been violently slain.

> It is there that the three kings were: Mac Cuill, Mac Cécht and Mac Gréne. They welcomed him, that is, Íth son of Bregon. Íth surpassed the judges of Ireland in cleverness and pleading, and he righted every complaint and contention that there was among them, and he said: 'Enact rightful law, for you dwell in a good land. Abundant are its acorns and honey and wheat and fish.

Balanced are its heat and cold.' Then they plotted to kill Íth, and they banished him from Ireland; and he departed from them in Ailech and came into Mag nÍtha. Emissaries followed him, and slew him there in Mag nÍtha . . .. And so it was to avenge Íth that the sons of Míl (that is, the Gaels) came; for Íth's corpse had been fetched to Spain.[20]

The text does not explain the sudden, murderous hostility of the three kings, but the most natural interpretation seems to be that Íth had made them jealous—shown himself, indeed, to be potentially a better ruler than they. His performance had demonstrated his possession of two qualities: first, that capacity for just judgment which was so central to the ideal of kingship; and second, the ability to pronounce the proper value of the various blessings of nature.

The supernatural dimension of kingship, and the close connection between the king and the land, are further reflected in another ancient symbolic concept. In the story of Íth, the three divine kings of Ireland have queens whose names are the names of the land: similarly, a mortal king was portrayed as the lover of a female figure who represented, or embodied, the territory over which he ruled. Several ideas are bound together within this potent image. Only when he has been accepted by the incarnate land is a man truly a rightful king; but she needs him as much as he needs her. In tale after tale, the 'woman of sovereignty' appears as a monstrous hag, a wandering madwoman or a ragged servant until her destined mate takes her to himself: but then, upon the instant, she is restored to youth, queenliness and beauty. Yet again, the true king's identity is revealed by his ability to bring forth the perfection latent within the natural world.

This scenario, the basic pattern of which can be traced through a multitude of variations, is often referred to as the 'king and goddess theme'. It is attested throughout the length and breadth of the Celtic world, from ancient times down virtually to the present, and has been repeatedly subjected to scholarly analysis.[21] In what follows, I shall consider only a few of the topic's many aspects.

Various modes of relationship are illustrated in these 'king and goddess' stories. The 'woman of sovereignty' may appear as the wife of a mortal king; but if this is the case, she herself will be portrayed as a mortal.[22] If she is a supernatural being, then she and the destined king will only enjoy a single, transient encounter:[23] if he tries to possess her as his permanent consort this attempt will ultimately fail, and his own death will be the likely consequence.[24] There are only two preconditions which will permit a lasting union between members of the divine and earthly races, neither of them compatible with the exercise of kingship: either the immortal spouse or lover must be kept a secret from the rest of the community,[25] or else her mortal partner must leave this world forever.[26] The king is marked by his link, vivid and intimate, with the divinity that indwells the land: but this connection gives him no rights over her, and will be likewise granted to all of his successors. The mortal and immortal spheres which have been conjoined in their embrace remain distinct, and counterposed.

Sexual union symbolises, and aspires to, an ideal of love, harmony and fruitfulness: an ideal which is here extended to the relationship between the ruler and the realm. But such a relationship, no less than the pairings of individual men and women, is susceptible of failure, and indeed of deliberate perversion. The literature of early Ireland is full of tales in which the king or would-be king is rejected by the 'woman of sovereignty', or in which he brutally abuses her. Let us consider an example of the latter.

The story called The Battle of Mag Mucrama begins in ancient Munster: Ailill is the king of the province, and Áine Chliach is a síd, or hollow hill inhabited by the immortals, near his royal stronghold.[27] On the night of Hallowe'en or Samain, when the visible and invisible spheres come together, Ailill arrogantly pastures his horses upon the hill: an act which, in early Irish law, was tantamount to a formal claim to possession.[28] The powers of the hill respond by stripping it of its grass, even as they might deprive the whole realm of its crops; but Ailill refuses to understand what is happening.

So it happened to him twice. He wondered at it. He sent off messengers to Ferches the poet . . .. He was a seer and a warrior. He came to speak to him. Both go one Samain night to the hill. Ailill remains on the hill. Ferches was aside from it. Sleep then comes to Ailill while listening to the grazing of the beasts. They came out of the *síd* with Eógabul son of Daurgabul king of the *síd* after them and Áine daughter of Eógabul with a bronze dulcimer in her hand playing before him. Ferches rises up to meet him and struck him. Eógabul ran on into the *síd*. Ferches attacks him with a great spear so that his back broke when he reached the *síd*.

Ailill had intercourse with the girl. While he was so engaged the woman sucked his ear so that she left neither flesh nor skin on it and none ever grew on it from that time. So that Ailill Bare-ear is his name since then. 'You have been wicked to me,' said Áine, 'in raping me and killing my father. I will do you violence on that account: I will leave no property in your possession when we part.'[29]

There are obscurities here, but the central ideas seem clear enough. The hill and the goddess have the same name—Áine—and are ultimately aspects of one another. The king's sins—grazing the sacred ground, and violating the woman of the *síd*—are likewise two aspects of a single sin, perceived on the natural and the supernatural planes. After he has raped Áine, Ailill has been himself disfigured: his outward appearance reflects the corruption of his kingship.[30]

For an account of a more auspicious union, we can turn to a tale first attested in a poem of the eleventh or twelfth century. Here we are told that four of the seven sons of Dáire, each of whom bore the name Lugaid, hunted a magical fawn; the destinies of their descendants were foreshadowed in the way in which the prey was divided, with the right to the fawn as a whole going to Lugaid Loígde. But this was not the only omen of the evening.

As the men sat there, beside the fire in the house, there came to them a hag, hideous the misfortune, harsh and bizarre.

She reared higher aloft than any mast of a ship; each of her ears was bigger than a hut for sleeping; blacker was her shape than any appearance—the hag weighed heavy on every heart.

The row of her teeth, come what may, was greater than a chessboard; her long nose projected further than the cold beam of a plough.

Each of the fists of the uncouth woman was bigger than a basket of ears of wheat; each of her rough black knees was bigger than a boulder on an embankment.

She had a swollen middle, as I know, without any ribs up to the armpits; her head was covered with scabs and thick lumps, and was as black as jet, like a mountain covered with furze . . ..

The nature of the tender lads changed as they faced that swollen, lecherous horror. Rather than look at her, they would have preferred to be buried alive.

Their sense and their judgment fled: this was something far beyond [the dangers of] combat. The sons of Dáire gave themselves up to a death of utter shame.

She addressed an ill saying to them: 'Let one of you sleep with me tonight; or else I will eat you all, both hounds and sturdy men'.

When he saw the evident danger, Lugaid Loígde said to them: 'I will sleep with her, a reluctant act. It is enough for you to lose me alone'.

As the firelight failed, she put herself into another strange form. She took on a shape with the glory of praise: she was rosy-skinned, with pointed breasts.

Such were her eyes . . . that three beams of the sun shone from each of them. Wherever she looked, it was bright.

The fair purple brooch slid down from her breasts, free of old age: you could have [seen to] crush a louse in that place, such was the radiance of her lovely skin.[31]

Then the lad asked her, 'Beautiful girl, whence do you come? Name your lineage, tell it now, speak to me and do not conceal'.

'I will tell you, tender lad. With me the high kings sleep. I am the slim graceful girl, the Kingship of Scotland and Ireland.

'To you I have shown myself tonight, but there will be nothing from our encounter. You will have a son, all the fairer: he is the boy with whom I shall sleep.'[32]

As I have already mentioned, we find this supernatural polarity expressed elsewhere as well. The 'woman of sovereignty' can be an epiphany either of beauty or of ugliness: she can be supremely desirable, or else a monstrosity so hideous as to threaten the sanity of those who see her, and deprive them of their will to live. In a story like the tale of Lugaid Loígde, the point of this symbolism is presumably to illustrate the concept that the land only flourishes under the rule of a rightful king: it is he who can bring cosmos out of chaos. But the image is also a reflection of the nature of phenomenal existence as a whole. The goddess is both beautiful and ugly, both benevolent and destructive, because she embodies a reality which transcends these opposites. Repeatedly in early Irish literature, and also in other Celtic sources, we can find traces of a doctrine that the goddess of the land and the goddess of war are one and the same: that fertility and slaughter, generation and destruction, are the contrasting faces of a unity. This is the essence of the world of flux, of time and becoming, over which the goddess presides.[33] The same duality of aspect can be observed elsewhere, notably in the various manifestations of the Great Goddess in India; or we can compare the eleventh chapter of the *Bhagavad Gītā*, in which Krishna grants to Arjuna a mind-shattering vision of his unveiled being, a manifold and unimaginable vastness which swallows all things in its myriad mouths.

It is this supernatural power, then, which the king confronts on behalf of the people: if he rules justly it is manifest as beauty and fruitfulness, but if he fails in his office it becomes a maelstrom of discordant energy which will destroy him. Whatever his fate may be, the same fate will be shared by his subjects: for good or ill, his individuality is the symbolic embodiment of their collective being.

The union between king and goddess seems in the old days to have been enacted in a public ritual, a ceremony comparable to the 'sacred marriage' attested in Mesopotamian and other religions.[34] As late as the fourteenth century, a chieftain's inauguration could still be referred to as a *banais ríghe*, a 'wedding of kingship';[35] and a visitor to Ireland in the late twelfth century gives a scandalised (and probably distorted) hearsay account of an inauguration in Donegal which involved the king-to-be copulating with a mare—easy enough to dismiss outright as a colonialist slur, but for the fact that a suggestive analogue can be cited from ancient India.[36] The kings of Tara would also assert their authority, once in each reign, by convening a great assembly with the suggestive name *feis Temro*, or 'wedding of Tara': the nuptial dimension is in this case further reflected in the tradition that this ceremonial affirmation of sovereignty could not be celebrated by 'a king without a queen'.[37]

The *feis Temro* was closely associated with the old religion. Its observance lapsed with the spread of Christianity, and an attempt to revive it in the mid-sixth century was shortly followed by the death of the officiating king and the permanent abandonment of the site of Tara itself. Later legends associated both events with the curses of the saints.[38] Certain fundamental aspects of the ideology of Irish kingship proved, throughout all the centuries of the old Gaelic order, difficult or impossible for the church to assimilate: it is noteworthy that, despite some early efforts in this direction, the inauguration of kings never acquired in Ireland the sacramental dimension which characterises it elsewhere in Europe.[39]

*

According to other traditions, the rightful king of Tara was validated not by a female incarnation of sovereignty, but by one or more inanimate talismans. We are told of a cloak kept at Tara which would only fit the true ruler, and of a chariot which only he could mount. He had then to drive the chariot between two stones, which would draw apart only for him; and over a stone named Fál at the end of the chariot-course, which would cry out in confirmation of his title. Only then would the people utter their own acclamation: 'Fál has accepted him!'[40]

There are two aspects of this account on which I would like to comment further. First, the chariot: the drive along the chariot-course which tests the candidate for kingship is clearly symbolic of his future reign. Even as the charioteer controls the brute strength of the horses, steering both beasts to a single goal, so the king must harmonise and direct the multitude of forces within his realm—the same image, applied to the integration of the individual soul, appears in Plato's *Phaedrus* and in the *Kaṭha Upaniṣad*.[41] The chariot, an aggregate of many parts which the skill of artisans has combined into a single vehicle, is another representation of the people unified in subjection to their ruler. A passage in *The Testament of Morand* reminds us of how fragile this unity can be, and of the king's responsibility for safeguarding it:

> Let him regard [his kingship like] the charioteer of an old chariot, for the charioteer of an old wheel-rim does not sleep. He looks ahead, he looks behind; in front and turning to the right and turning to the left. He looks, he defends, he gives protection, so that he may not break the wheel-rims which run under him either by neglect or by violence.[42]

The series of kingship tests culminates with the stone Fál, which cries out when the wheel of the chariot passes over it. This stone is mentioned in several other sources as one of the wonders of Tara: it is usually the touch of the king's foot which evokes its shout of affirmation. According to the *Book of Taking*, the gods brought it with them from the 'northern islands of the world' when they came to Ireland in the clouds of the air;[43] and an older text likewise hints at its Otherworldly origins.[44] Like other pagan oracles, Fál is said to have fallen silent at the birth of Christ. The doctrine that it was taken to Scotland in the sixth century—remaining there to become the famous Stone of Scone which was brought to London in 1296, and only returned to Scotland seven centuries later—is first attested in the later Middle Ages, and evidently reflects no more than Scottish wishful thinking:[45] the stone was still at Tara in the later

tenth century, when the poet Cinaed ua hArtucán composed a
quatrain expressing its symbolic identity with Ireland as a whole:

> The stone on which my two heels rest:
> from it the island of Fál is named.
> Between the two coasts of a vigorous flood,
> 'Plain of Fál' is upon all Ireland.[46]

The stone's present whereabouts, however, are not known.

Fál, which cries out when stepped upon by the rightful king, is
only the most prominent example of a pervasive association of
Celtic kingship with the foot. Rather than being crowned, an Irish
king would ceremonially put on a single shoe, having come to the
inauguration with one foot bare; or else the shoe would be thrown
over the new king's head 'whilst he sate in his stoane chayer upon
the hyll'.[47] Welsh legend speaks of kings disguising themselves as
shoemakers, a motif which seems to have resonances with the cult
of the ancient Celtic deity Lugus;[48] and of one legendary king who
could only live while his feet rested in the lap of a maiden who
seems to have symbolised the unviolated earth.[49] The importance of
the king's foot is reflected especially clearly in Edmund Spenser's
View of the State of Ireland, written in 1595:

> They used to place him that shall be their captain upon a stone
> always reserved for that purpose, and placed commonly upon a
> hill; in some of which I have seen formed and engraven a foot,
> which they say was the measure of their first captain's foot,
> whereon he, standing, received an oath to preserve all the ancient
> former customs of the country inviolable ... and then hath a
> wand delivered unto him by him whose proper office that is;
> after which, descending from the stone, he turneth himself
> round, thrice forward and thrice backward.[50]

Other aspects of the royal ideal are also important, such as generosity and courage: much could be said about these as well, but

nearly all of it would be closely parallel to what is found in a myriad other cultures. The image with which I would like to close is this one: the king with his foot upon the rock. However much he may be exalted above his fellows, he owes his status to his contact with the ground: it is this contact which most essentially defines him. The ultimate confirmation of his authority is a voice crying from the earth.

NOTES

1. For a summary discussion of different aspects of Irish legendary history, the reader may consult J. Carey, *The Irish National Origin-Legend: Synthetic Pseudohistory* (Cambridge, 1994); and *idem*, 'Native elements in Irish pseudohistory' in *Cultural Identity and Cultural Integration: Ireland and Europe in the Early Middle Ages*, ed. Doris Edel, (Dublin, 1995), 45–60 (presented as a lecture at the Temenos Academy, 31 January 1994).

2. *De Bello Gallico* i.1. I have touched upon the connections between the Fir Bolg and the Belgae in 'Fir Bolg: a native etymology revisited', *Cambridge Medieval Celtic Studies* xvi (1988) 77–83.

3. Some of these comparanda are discussed by Alwyn and Brinley Rees, *Celtic Heritage: Ancient Tradition in Ireland and Wales* (London and New York, 1961), 148–51, 385–6.

4. Slightly adapted from my translation in John T. Koch and John Carey, eds, *The Celtic Heroic Age: Literary Sources for Ancient Celtic Europe and Early Ireland and Wales* (3rd ed.: Oakville CT and Aberystwyth, 2001), 248–50. Cf. R. A. S. Macalister, ed. and trans., *Lebor Gabála Érenn*, 5 vols (London, 1938–56), iv. 8–45, 52–61.

5. Siegmund Hellmann, ed., *Pseudo-Cyprianus De XII Abusivis Saeculi*, Texte und Untersuchungen xxxiv (Leipzig, 1909), 51–3. This work exercised a significant influence on the development of ideas concerning kingship in western Europe generally: see H. H. Anton, 'Pseudo-Cyprian *De duodecim abusiuis saeculi* und sein Einfluß auf den Kontinent, insbesondere auf die karolingischen Fürstenspiegel', in *Die Iren und Europa im früheren Mittelalter*, ed. Heinz Löwe, 2 vols (Stuttgart, 1982), ii.568–617.

6. For some examples, see the index to John Carey, *King of Mysteries: Early Irish Religious Writings* (2nd ed.: Dublin, 2000).

7. Joseph Vendryes, *Lexique étymologique de l'irlandais ancien*, Lettres R S (Dublin and Paris, 1974), s.v.

8. Liam Breatnach, 'Ardri as an old compound', *Ériu* xxxvii (1986) 192–3; cf. J. Carey, 'The rhetoric of Echtrae Chonlai', *Cambrian Medieval Celtic Studies* xxx (1995) 41–65: p. 56 n. 66.

9. Text in James Carney, ed. and trans., *The Poems of Blathmac son of Cú Brettan* (London, 1964), 36–40 (my translation).

10. M. A. O'Brien, ed., *Corpus Genealogiarum Hiberniae* (Dublin, 1962), p. 1.

11. 'The Ecology of Miracles', in *A Single Ray of the Sun: Religious Speculation in Early Ireland* (Andover and Aberyswyth, 1999), 39–73 (based on a lecture presented at the Temenos Academy, 16 February 1998).

12. Carey, *King of Mysteries*, 52–3.

13. For considerations pointing to this dating see J. Carey, 'On the interrelationships of some *Cín Dromma Snechtai* texts', *Ériu* xlvi (1995) 71–92: pp. 86–9.

14. Text in Fergus Kelly, ed. and trans., *Audacht Morainn* (Dublin, 1976), 6 (my translation).

15. *Odyssey* xix.108–14, *Works and Days* 225–47.

16. *Rig Veda* i.105.12.

17. Kelly, op. cit., 10–14.

18. *Genesis* 1:27–8, 2:19.

19. *Ab Urbe Condita* v.34.1–5.

20. Koch and Carey, *Celtic Heroic Age*, 263; cf. Macalister, *Lebor Gabála Érenn*, v.16–20. For a linguistic argument that the figure of Íth is of great antiquity see John T. Koch, 'Ériu, Alba, and Letha: When was a language ancestral to Gaelic first spoken in Ireland?', *Emania* ix (1991) 17–27: pp. 22–3.

21. Two pioneering essays which remain valuable are T. F. O'Rahilly, 'On the origin of the names Érainn and Ériu', *Ériu* xiv (1946) 7–28, and R. A. Breatnach, 'The lady and the king: a theme of Irish literature', *Studies* xlii (1953) 321–36; important recent contributions are the articles of Kim McCone, 'Fírinne agus torthúlacht', *Léachtaí Cholm Cille* xi (1980) 136–73, and Máire Herbert, 'Goddess and king: The sacred marriage in early Ireland', in *Women and Sovereignty* ed. L. O. Fradenburg, (Edinburgh, 1992), 264–75. See further Ananda K. Coomaraswamy, 'On the loathly bride', *Speculum* xx (1945) 391–404. For some euhemerised examples from pre-Christian Celtic tradition see Koch and Carey, *Celtic Heroic Age*, 38–42.

22. A particularly clear example is provided by Eithne the wife of Cormac mac Airt, especially as she is described in the tales *Esnada Tige Buchet* (ed. and trans. Whitley Stokes, 'The Songs of Buchet's House', *Revue Celtique* xxv [1904] 18–38, 225–7) and 'Cormac's Dream' (ed. and trans. James Carney, 'Nia son of Lugna Fer Trí', *Éigse* ii [1940] 187–97). Even figures such as Medb, Mór Muman, and the Old Woman of Beare, who form unions with a sequence of kings which may extend across generations, are not identified as supernatural beings in the sources.

23. This is for example the case in the tale *Echtra Mac nEchach Mugmedóin* (Koch and Carey, *Celtic Heroic Age*, 203–8); and in the Welsh folktale translated ibid., 355.

24. Examples occur in the tales *Tochmarc Étaíne* (Koch and Carey, *Celtic Heroic Age*, 146–65), *Tochmarc Becfola* (ed. and trans. Máire Bhreathnach, 'A new edition of *Tochmarc Becfhola*', *Ériu* xxxv [1984] 59–91); and *Aided Muirchertaig meic Erca* (ed. and trans. Whitley Stokes, 'The Death of Muirchertach mac Erca', *Revue Celtique* xxiii [1902] 395–437; here the enchantress Sín has herself been partly euhemerised).

25. As in *Ces Noínden* (ed. and trans. Vernam Hull, 'Noínden Ulad: The Debility of the Ulidians', *Celtica* viii [1968] 1–42: p. 37).

26. The most celebrated instance, and one of the earliest surviving Irish tales, is *Echtrae Chonnlai* (ed. and trans. Kim McCone, *Echtrae Chonnlai and the Beginnings of Vernacular Narrative Writing in Ireland* [Maynooth, 2000]). That the two preconditions were conjoined in Breton tradition appears to be reflected in the lays of Graelent (ed. and trans. Alexandre Micha, *Lais féeriques des XIIe et XIIIe siècles* [Paris, 1992], 18–61) and Lanval (ed. Jean Rychner, *Les lais de Marie de France* [Paris, 1978], 72–92).

27. In other sources, the hill itself is the site of such a stronghold: references in Edmund Hogan, *Onomasticon Goedelicum* (Dublin and London, 1910), 20–1.

28. Thus the legal text *Din Techtugud* states that 'landed property has been recovered by means of high occupation through the labours of horses who extended it, and it was a joining across borders' (trans. Calvert Watkins, 'Indo-European metrics and archaic Irish verse', *Celtica* vi [1963] 194–249: p. 221; cf. D. A. Binchy, ed., *Corpus Iuris Hibernici* [Dublin, 1978], 205).

29. This is a slightly modified version of the translation which accompanies the edition by Máirín O Daly, *Cath Maige Mucrama: The Battle of Mag Mucrama* (London, 1975), 39. For further commentary on this scene see Tomás Ó Cathasaigh, 'The theme of *lommrad* in *Cath Maige Mucrama*', *Éigse* xviii.2 (1981) 211–24.

30. That it is specifically the ear which is affected may symbolise the destruction of Ailill's good reputation. For the connection between satire and physical assaults upon the ear, cf. Vernam Hull, 'Miscellanea: 4. The ancient Irish practice of rubbing the earlap as a means of coercion', *Zeitschrift für celtische Philologie* xxi (1939) 324–9.

31. This rather mundane way of describing exceptionally good lighting recurs elsewhere in medieval Irish literature: thus J. J. Tierney, ed. and trans., *Dicuili Liber de Mensura Orbis Terrae* (Dublin, 1967), 74–5.

32. Text in E. J. Gwynn, ed. and trans., *The Metrical Dindshenchas*, 5 vols (Dublin, 1903–35), iv.138–42 (my translation). Another version of the story, which may preserve some older features, occurs in Whitley Stokes, ed. and trans., 'Cóir Anmann: Fitness of Names', *Irische Texte* iii.2 (1897) 285–444: pp. 316–23.

33. I have discussed this question in greater detail in 'Notes on the Irish war-goddess', *Éigse* xix.2 (1983) 263–75.

34. See for instance the discussion by Thorkild Jacobsen, *The Treasures of Darkness: A History of Mesopotamian Religion* (New Haven and London, 1976), 32–47.

35. Thus A. Martin Freeman, ed. and trans., *Annála Connacht: The Annals of Connacht* (A.D. 1224–1544) (Dublin, 1944), *sub anno* 1310; and cf. the account of a *banais taísighechta* 'wedding of chieftainship' celebrated in 1475, in John O'Donovan, ed. and trans., *Annála Ríoghachta Éireann: Annals of the Kingdom of Ireland by the Four Masters*, 7 vols (2nd ed.: Dublin, 1856), iv.1090–3.

36. Gerald of Wales, *The History and Topography of Ireland*, trans. John J. O'Meara (rev. imp.: Harmondsworth, 1982), 109–10. The analogy with the Indian horse sacrifice or a_vamedha (in which however the mating was only mimicked) has been discussed by Franz Rolf Schröder, 'Ein altirischer Krönungsritus und das indogermanische Rossopfer', *Zeitschrift für celtische Philologie* xvi (1927) 310–12.

37. This statement is found in the tale *Tochmarc Étaíne* (Koch and Carey, *Celtic Heroic Age*, 154).

38. The most comprehensive discussion is that of D. A. Binchy, 'The fair of Tailtiu and the feast of Tara', *Ériu* xviii (1958) 113–38.

39. Cf. the remarks of Francis John Byrne, *Irish Kings and High-Kings* (London, 1973), 21–2, 255–6; and Michael J. Enright's study *Iona, Tara and Soissons: The Origin of the Royal Anointing Ritual* (Berlin and New York, 1985).

40. The description is given in Lucius Gwynn, ed. and trans., 'De Shíl Chonairi Móir',

Ériu vi (1912) 130–43; for the proposed emendation of Gwynn's rendering of a crucial phrase in this text see J. Carey, 'Varia I. *Ferp cluche*', ibid. 1 (1999) 165–8.

41. *Phaedrus* 246ab; *Kaṭha Upaniṣad* iii.3–9.

42. Kelly, *Audacht Morainn*, p. 8 (my translation).

43. Koch and Carey, *Celtic Heroic Age*, 252–3; cf. Macalister, *Lebor Gabála Érenn* iv.108–13, 142–5, 168–75.

44. Rudolf Thurneysen, ed. and trans., 'Baile in Sc_il', *Zeitschrift für celtische Philologie* xx (1936) 213–27: p. 219; English paraphrase in Myles Dillon, *The Cycles of the Kings* (repr.: Dublin, 1994), 12.

45. This identification was also subscribed to by the patriotic Irish historian Geoffrey Keating in the seventeenth century, perhaps on account of the hopes which the Gaels of Ireland were then pinning on the house of Stuart: David Comyn and P. S. Dinneen, ed. and trans., *Foras Feasa ar Éirinn: The History of Ireland by Geoffrey Keating, D.D.*, 4 vols (London, 1902–14), i.206–9. The ceremonial restoration of the Stone to Scotland took place on 30 November 1996.

46. Macalister, *Lebor Gabála Érenn* iv.244 (my translation). For an indication that the stone was in fact still at Tara in the late twelfth century see Brian Ó Cuív, 'A poem in praise of Raghnall, king of Man', *Éigse* viii (1956–7) 283–301: p. 299.

47. M. A. O'Brien, 'Short notes', *Celtica* ii (1952–4) 350–3: pp. 351–3; Proinsias Mac Cana, 'The topos of the single sandal in Irish tradition', ibid. x (1973) 160–6: pp. 160–2.

48. Rachel Bromwich, ed. and trans., *Trioedd Ynys Prydein: The Welsh Triads* (2nd ed.: Cardiff, 1978), 176–8.

49. Ifor Williams, ed., *Pedeir Keinc y Mabinogi* (2nd ed.: Caerdydd, 1951), 67, with translation in Gwyn and Thomas Jones, *The Mabinogion* (London, 1949), 55. Cf. J. Carey, 'A British myth of origins?', *History of Religions* xxxi (1991) 24–38: pp. 30–3.

50. Henry Morley, ed., *Ireland under Elizabeth and James I* (London, 1890), 42.

JOHN S. ALLITT
THE THEMES OF NOBILITY & MONARCHY IN DANTE'S THOUGHT

Dante's political thought has fascinated generations. For example, the *De Monarchia* was once considered a dangerous document and was placed on the Index. Generations of Italian nationalists have interpreted the *Commedia* as an esoteric document to be decoded for the benefit of their country.

Too often the popular approach to Dante remains on levels that ignore the fact that the poet's life was essentially a spiritual pilgrimage—an inner journey brought about by his meeting at an early age with a young Florentine girl. From that point of time on, Dante tells us that life took on a deeper significance; his major writings acquired a confessional quality. He desired over the years to understand the deep change that was taking place within him. In this he was continuing a tradition that had originated with one of his mentors, St Augustine.

It is enough to read the first few pages of the *Vita Nuova* to know that Dante was deeply, and profoundly, moved by the act of *seeing* his beloved Beatrice. His beholding had been nothing less than an epiphany. Life could never be the same again. Something had irreversibly changed deep within him. His awareness, consciousness of life was propped up, as it were, by the significance of the figure of womanhood. Whatever befell him, from success to failure, from wandering the streets of Florence to the bitterness of exile, the image awoken within him by Beatrice would simply not go away or leave him to get on with his life as do other men. He was to carry the icon of her radiant beauty for life. All things related to her in some way or another, from the political to the spiritual.

*

Dante studies are a minefield, especially when one attempts to give order to the major works. Here I follow the traditionally accepted sequence of the main writings. It is my intention to observe the poet's development of thought regarding the political world, especially the themes of nobility and monarchy. To have considered only the De Monarchia, written during his exile, would have been to ignore the development and thread of thought which unifies the entire opus. I will thus move on to the Vita Nuova, and to the Convivio, look briefly at De vulgari eloquentia, consider the De Monarchia, and find rest, ultimately, in the Commedia.

It is a vast panorama and here I have to press on from book to book without being tempted to relate the many fascinating but time-consuming insights and problems that generations of scholars have set before the student of Dante and his work.

La Vita Nuova

Moses before the Burning Bush removed his shoes. Dante before Beatrice experienced disturbance in his heart, mind and guts. He was physically ill at the shock of beholding beauty revealed through the grace of the feminine. Meetings, indeed simply the act of seeing Beatrice, could weaken him and cause him to dream extraordinary dreams. His psychosomatic make up, the very quality of his soul, had been changed.[1] His intellect had been drawn to a focal point. The significance of Beatrice, the search for meaning in daily affairs, his political aspirations, his relationship to a Church that meddled all too readily with secular, political power, even the Divinity itself, were all drawn through the circumference of his consciousness, and struggled for equilibrium at the centre of his soul. It seemed as if Beatrice had summoned him to be and to become through her; she was the gateway to understanding and knowing his real self.

As Love revealed Himself to the young poet, so was he given good advice; for example, he was not to ask for more than that which was useful to him, non dimandar più che utile ti sia.[2] He was to give up playing intellectual games and come to the crux of the matter: figli mi, tempus est ut praetermittantur simulacra nostra.[3] He had to acknowledge that his inner life was as insecure as a wobbly wheel. Love said to him, 'I am the centre to which all parts of the circumference are equal, but with you this is not so'. (*Ego tamquam centrum circuli, cui simili modo se habent circumferentiae partes, tu autem non sic.*[4]) And so he wobbled along through life. There was no part of the circumference of his consciousness that did not ultimately relate to the power of womanhood.

He struggled to understand the political and religious worlds, but too easily he identified himself with this and that, over there, then here, and again over there, and so on. He was centre-less.

Dante had, however, grasped the deep symbolic significance of the circle. It would become the essential structure of the *Commedia*. Whether we consider his descent into Hell, the climbing of Purgatory or the ascent of the Heavens, the circle is the governing symbolic structure.

Amidst the humdrum of his daily life the poet soon stumbled across the uncompromising fact of Free Will. It was his misuse of Free Will that made the wheel of his consciousness wobble off the true road into the ditches, the brambles and eventually the Dark Wood leading to Hell.

If one turns the pages of the *Purgatorio* and finds the central cantos, there, half way through the hundred cantos of the *Commedia* we find Dante, Marco Lombardo and Virgil discussing Free Will. Free Will according to Dante is at the heart of human consciousness. We are totally free to make what we wish of ourselves.

The poet observed with an acute eye the religious and secular worlds about him, and recognised that they were rotten because of the misuse of the will. They willed not the good, nor the true or the beautiful. There was no real desire for justice or even a genuine peace among the nations.

*

Beatrice married another and died young; Florence, his own city-state, betrayed him, twisted justice and exiled him. The Empire had been reduced to impotency and Italy was a nation divided between squabbling factions and warring families. Worse still the Papacy betrayed supernatural justice at a drop of a hat due to its relentless grasping for political power.

The bitter exile had begun.

*

Il Convivio

Dante throughout his life considered himself a citizen of Florence, and the medieval Italian city-state (*civitas*) is the root of his political thought. A person without *civic* responsibilities would lack, therefore, in Dante's mind, the basic qualities appertaining to his status as a member of the human family. The city was an essential centre of awareness. The city walls were the circumference excluding the profane and, at the same time, enclosing a social world.

> Fiorenza dentro de la cerchia antica
> . . . si stava in pace, sobria e pudica.[5]
>
> (Florence within her ancient circle
> . . . lived in peace, sober and chaste.)

A city is like a *mandala* of consciousness with its churches, seats of learning, the bustle of social and family life. In a city goods and raw materials have to be turned to success and crafted into things of worth. To expand a city only for the sake of wealth and sudden riches was for Dante a cause of degeneration. The flow of the city's daily life should not be a social game of false pretence; a city's conduct should be grounded in right *mores*, right *moeurs*. Strife must cease between families, for right-living brings about concord and stability. Thus to be a good citizen is the essential step for a man. He is by nature a political animal and is forced into social relationship. A city's citizens should seek to be an expression of the 'good life', right awareness; be morally upright, conscious of the distinction between right and wrong.

For Dante having known Beatrice meant to appreciate the embodiment of such social blessings. She had revealed herself to him in the bustle and flow of civic life and was therefore for the young poet the embodiment of all that was good in Florence. Just as the effigies of Britannia, Fortune or an Empress are minted on coins, so she was stamped on his heart. Beatrice was his true currency of worth. Without knowing Beatrice the city, or any city for that matter, cannot hope to have a profound significance.

Beatrice as a messenger of the higher worlds is the instrumental epiphany that leads on to the ultimate revelation, that is, from Florence to the heavenly Jerusalem. To know Beatrice is not a static, narcissistic consciousness, but the dynamic, leading her lover onwards through the ever-changing scenes of life. Furthermore, it is the role of Beatrice to lead on to the fullness of the feminine mysteries and consequently to the Lord Himself. A society without Beatrice is without the Lord; such a society can be but an expression of the city of the damned, those who have lost the good of the intellect.

If Beatrice is sought, then justice and peace will be the hallmark of the city. Justice and peace come from the good sap of the root of human nature. Hence to seek Beatrice is to desire the 'good life'. She, like the statue above the law courts or Victory riding in her chariot above the gateways of cities, is the substratum for the right use of reason. To know Beatrice is essential when setting up a seat of authority. To grasp for power by the force of arms is wrong. The *Convivio* states: '. . . the Roman power was acquired not by reason nor by decree of universal consent, but by force, which seems to be the contrary of reason'.[6] The use of brutal force is contrary to reason when applied to the city and civic life. The key to true civic life is to be centred in the feminine mysteries for only thus will it become receptive to the good, and make decisions in the light of truth, and be aware of beauty.

St Augustine's *Civitas Dei* had taught Dante to observe how a city, be it Florence or Bologna, Falmouth or Birmingham, depends on drawing its model from the Heavenly City. This, like the Rose of Paradise, has Mary, the Mother of God enthroned, and Beatrice waiting on her pleasure. This act of drawing inspiration from the true model or archetype is the primary imperative of *la vera città*; without it the city degenerates into the *civitas diaboli*, the city of the damned.

*

Exile from Florence on trumped-up charges forced Dante to take account of the spirit of negativity, typical of the city of the damned. However he never lost his ideal of the *libera civitas*, the free city. He considered the city to be the footstool upon which nations must rest. Put another way, Dante implies that the family rooted within civic life, is responsible to and for the social flow of the city (town or village); it is the basis of the good life. National governments may pronounce all the edicts they want, but without the substratum of a happy and good civic life, all will be to no avail. These essential qualities he took for granted as grafted into the Christian life and dependent on a right, enlightened education.

And so it was that his understanding of Beatrice evolved into her becoming the Lady of Philosophy, the Lady who taught men to love wisdom, saving them from descent into the lust, violent pride and avarice of the infernal city.

Let us look forward to the *Commedia* for a moment and stand on the shores of the island upon which rests Mount Purgatory. Beneath us, deep in the abyss, lies the cracked, ruptured City of Dis, the *civitas diaboli*; high above on the Mountain's summit is the Garden of Earthly Innocence. To reach the Garden and to be re-united there with Beatrice requires much effort, indeed the will of our total self. There can be no compromise. The lofty Mountain symbolises the purifying effort required to rid ourselves of the marks of sin; only thus may right-contemplation be achieved. Beatrice is nowhere to be seen along the island's shores. There is, however, an old man, Cato of Uttica. He was in life a pagan and represents in Dante's imagery the moral imperative, the cardinal virtues and true Philosophy, the love of wisdom—qualities of life which are set before pagan and Christian alike.

Note that by the end of his life, Dante's thought had significantly developed. He no longer over-values Philosophy, though it is most certainly the foundation from which the journey of return may be embraced. The natural moral virtues guard the isle upon which the Mountain of purification rests. God is not mocked; the co-operation of our will is essential, but philosophy alone cannot get us to the Garden of Earthly Innocence. Our change of consciousness, our *metanoia*, does not remove us from our body or the natural world. It rather calls us to embrace the fruits of redemption. Philosophy thus evolves in Dante's thought into theology, because the pilgrim soul must learn the way of prayer and contemplation.

This forward glance at the *Commedia* has served to indicate that Dante never felt his own affairs to be more important than the good estate of right-living.

It is obvious that right-education is essential for the regaining of the good life. We have to seek *perfezione di propia natura in ciascuna cosa*, perfection of our true nature in everything.[7] This is the basis of true *nobility*; it is a way open to all. To embrace such a way implies a maturing in *gentilezza, cortesia, virtù*—the qualities of nobility. In the *Purgatorio* the reader is told that worldly titles cease and all know each other by their Christian names, through courtesy and recognising the Christ in the other. Dante rejected Emperor Rudolph of Swabia's definition of nobility in that it consisted in 'ancient wealth and gracious manners'. Nobility for Dante did not lie in lineage or riches. Those of ancient lineage may often be base in spirit to the extent that they may be described as 'dead' even whilst yet alive, because for Dante to renounce the good of the intellect is death. He considered that a false understanding of the nature of nobility results from a diseased mind. Nobility is not a life of evil habits, a lack of intellect, entrenched false opinion, wrong judgements, unjust reverence and vilifying. Such falsity breeds the 'worst confusion in the world'.

Nobility for the poet is thus the perfection of our nature through the civic life. True nobility is to be recognised by its fruits. Following Aristotle, he lists eleven essential qualities:

1. *Courage*—for it controls rashness and timidity.
2. *Temperance*—for it controls indulgence and abstinence.
3. *Liberality*—for it controls our giving and receiving.
4. *Magnificence*—for it teaches how we incur expense and likewise how to limit it.
5. *Magnanimity*—moderates and acquires honour and reputation.
6. *Love of honour*—should moderate and order us regarding worldly honour.
7. *Mansuetude, gentleness*—moderates anger and the lack of patience, and teaches us not to be over-patient with evils as they confront us.
8. *Affability*—an essential quality for it makes us convivial and companionable.
9. *Truthfulness*—prevents us in our conversation from pretending to be more or less than we are.
10. *Pleasantness*—sets us free to make a proper and easy use of amusement. Dante uses the word *sollazia* thereby implying the solace gained through the right use of leisure.
11. *Justice*—constrains us to love and practice directness in all things.

These eleven fruits are the true marks of the soul engaged in the noble life; they are the largesse of right-living. They are to be found in the temporal blessedness of life; that is, they are the proper use of our energy, fulfilling our role in civic life, our vocation to be and guide us to right action. They 'paint' our true effigy by helping us to regain the likeness unto the Creator that has been disfigured by sin.

Beatrice as the focal point of the feminine mysteries is the embodiment of all these fruits and calls her lovers to embrace the same. They should be found in the life of the city, that of the Emperor and the Pope. In this, the life of Christ fulfilling the Beatitudes is the *forma*, the model for all.

Alas, we have betrayed such a high vocation.

*

De Vulgari Eloquentia and relevant Letters
on the theme of monarchy

Exile was a total humiliation. Dante was denied the civic life of the city he so loved and considered essential to maturity. He could understand and accept Beatrice's death as God's will, but to experience the treachery of the city he loved was quite other.

However, without the bitterness and hardships of exile it is possible that the Commedia would never have been written, at least with the contents as they are now known to posterity. Exile encouraged in Dante a growing sense of nationality; he could no longer retreat behind the comforting circumference of Florence's city walls. There was forced on him a widening and a maturing of his understanding of citizenship for all men, because through their humanity they are forced to relate to each other. Quoting Pythagoras, he insisted that it is through friendship that the many are made one. He also cites a Greek proverb that endorsed his Franciscan outlook on life: 'All things are common between friends'.

The great tragedy was that the Church of Rome had shown itself to be corrupt; the popes wielded the sword of political power; they were ruthless, without moral principles, the whole establishment merited judgement. It had strayed into the profane and had ignored its sacred duties. And so it was that the Empire as the rightful field for political struggle now became his hope. It was in its highest calling the seat of authority commissioned to restore justice and peace amidst the petty warring city-states of the Peninsular.

But how was it possible to give Italy a sense of unity? Any concept of nationhood seemed impossible with the many divided city-states, warring families and intriguing clerics, all at loggerheads, exasperating each other with the cacophony of their manifold dialects. His nation needed a seat of authority that would command respect. Furthermore its peoples deserved to discover the power of their own vernacular. It was easier for a Florentine to communicate with a Bergamasque in Latin than to attempt to use the Florentine vernacular. If in the future there was to be progress towards a united nation, then the Florentines and Bergamasques would have to learn to communicate in a common, mutually understandable vernacular, that is through the elegance of a living language and not the gabble of incomprehensible dialects.

Dante foresaw that the growth of the vernacular could compensate his nation by giving it at least a sense of unity. The promise of a vernacular Italian was the *luce nuova*, the *sole nuovo* and there was no greater force for the good in this than the art of poetry and song.

Dante, in common with modern scholars, recognised the genius of Italian poetry as originating with the Sicilian school of Frederick II. His evolving ideas concerning monarchy, he considered, also had a beginning with Frederick. The role of the monarch was to draw out of the *substantia humanae naturae*, the essence of human nature, that which is most excellent, the pursuit of *gentilezza*. Poetry was essential to this for it taught the right-use of language and groomed the intellect and the emotions. Such *nobilità* of the heart had in turn to focus itself on an authority like the *radii* of a circle uniting in a common central point.

As Dante considered the role of monarchy, he was increasingly drawn to Byzantium as his model, the Emperor Justinian in particular, for he had been the source of law. The function of the monarch was essentially to provide law and justice as the foundation of the empire. Indeed the basic human need for law justifies the monarch, *lo fondamento radicale de la imperiale maestade . . . è la necessità de la umana civiltade*. Thus, the role of the monarch is intellectually justified as the focal point for justice and peace among citizens. Dante had thus drawn together two of his prime sources, Aristotle (justice) and St Augustine (peace). The true empire was a theocracy.

There is more. The Nativity of Christ had indicated the chosen role of Rome in world history, she was the *santa cittade*, and had a duty towards the sacred. However, certain popes had turned from their duty through seeking political power; this had chained them to the three great sins of the *civitas diaboli*; lust, pride and avarice. Boniface VIII (1294–1303)[8] and Clement V (1305–1314)[9] were Dante's particular *bêtes noires*. He abhorred all who used papal supremacy to political ends as well as those who justified papal political claims by falsifying the teaching of the Church. For example, he despised the so-called Donation of Constantine, the spurious document (but unknown to Dante as being bogus) which maintained that Constantine had given to the pope political rule in Italy.

The monarch increasingly became in Dante's mind the only hope for justice and peace throughout the Peninsular, because he alone could draw the city-states into some sort of union. He saw Henry IV's Italian expedition of 1310 increasingly in prophetic terms. Henry would, like the Hound of Heaven, chase corruption underground to the abyss.[10] Dante damned his fellow Florentines for turning against Henry, and portrayed his beloved city as a viper to be crushed with the argument that all power comes from God and that the emperor (or monarch) was the minister of God; to resist him was to resist divine providence. In the light of the advent of Christ there were two essential authorities, St Peter and Caesar. They were like the sun and moon, the pope was the father of fathers and the emperor was the son of the Church, responsible for the good estate of his nations.

Henry died shortly after being crowned emperor in 1313, shattering Dante's dreams. After all, it is only fair to say that he had hoped that a purified Florence would have revoked his exile.

De Monarchia

We have already anticipated many themes to be found in the *De Monarchia*. The book was written after the death of Henry IV, *circa* 1316–17. Dante was then fully involved with the *Commedia* and contemplating the corruption of Church and State.[11] His despair with the political conflict and the sham all about him is echoed in words of Jeremiah which he quoted more than once in his works: *O vos omnes qui transitis per viam, attendite et videte si est dolor sicut dolor meus.* 'Is it nothing to you, all ye that pass by? Behold, and see if there be any sorrow like unto my sorrow.' The Biblical role of Jeremiah serves to emphasise the prophetic role adopted by the poet. He saw clearly that the tragic circumstances about him were due to humanity's departure from the Way, the Truth and the Life set as an example by the Lord Incarnate. For Dante ignorance of that which is known intuitively and intellectually as right can but bring about social and personal judgement, *crisis*. Thus it had to be the case that all human beings are endowed by God with the love of truth (*amorem veritatis*), surely it was the wish and duty to pass on that which has been received, from those who proceeded them to the new generation.

Dante argues, as ever in his works, from the axiom of Tradition, the revelations, insights and teachings that had been known to be enduring from generation to generation. His critics accused him of meddling, as being a new Uzzah, figuratively stretching out his hand to steady the tottering Ark[12]. No, he replied, he only sought to correct the course of the oxen.[13] The Ark was not his to touch[14]. His task was to reveal and to emphasise relevant aspects of matters true. Few were more important than the essential model (*forma*) for governing and ruling the nations of the world, the *temporalis monarchia*, the *imperium*—that is, the sovereign authority set over all others in secular time. His argument is not his own, he emphasised, but it was to be understood in the light of God.

Monarchy is set in this secular world amidst the ravages of *chronos*. It is a channel that derives its justification from the eternal worlds. Every truth that is not a first principle has to be demonstrated with reference to the truth of some first principle, and this Dante proposed to explore and to set out in his *De Monarchia*.

The subject of monarchy is intimately related to the political domain. Therefore, it is not theoretical but concerned with action. It is not speculative and yet the speculative enlightens our understanding of the secular, for right-action ultimately depends on right-contemplation. The spiritual quest, for example, does not find rest until it finds peace in the divine will—for in His will, is our peace. Thus the goal of the secular world must likewise be peace—universal peace, *pax universalis*. All our secular tasks and consequent energies must be directed towards this end. 'Behold, how good and how pleasant it is for brethren to dwell together in unity!' (Psalm 133)

Universal peace is therefore the task of each and every one of us.

The resources of the good of humanity must aim at this goal. All of us are endowed with the gift of intellect; it is incumbent upon each person to use the resources of his or her intellect for the good of the community in which they find themselves. This collaboration of intellects enables the human race to acquire from the first principles of knowledge new forms of intelligible knowledge; for example, a right-understanding of the role of monarchy. Such knowledge is not achievable by one person or a group of persons but only if it exists as a body of knowledge shared by all. Philosophical principles, that is the 'love of wisdom', are universal and necessary for the good estate of society, for peace. Such 'possible knowledge' indicates that every individual is responsible for his or her self—just as is a father for his family, an elected chairman for a committee or commune, a mayor for a city, a prime minister for a government, a monarch for a nation and the emperor as a focal point of nations. The emperor as understood by Dante must be by definition totally free from self-interest, free to channel right power down the manifold channels of hierarchy to the principles that govern the everyday in secular life.

The universal community, as envisaged by Dante, depends on an emperor who is free from the taints of the secular world (lust, violence, and avarice[15]) to mediate to others what we may well describe as Traditional Wisdom, a Solomon without the corruption of riches. The special task of all (opus proprium) is the building up of the richness and health of this 'possible intellect', for it directs us towards universal understanding and peace. There can be no pax universalis without such a universal human community. If there is no peace between men and the nations then there is no opportunity for a person to develop his aptitude for discovering truth, and climb to the highest rung which is the ultimate goal set before us all. Such is social action, not speculation. If we want peace we must strive for such a community of peoples and for this to come about the model (forma), idea, ideal, archetype, must first exist in the minds of people. That is, a right understanding of the role of monarchy. Thus, we might emphasise a fact Dante took for granted, which is that a right-education is essential for the growth and development of his ideal community.

Now Dante was, and still is, accused by certain critics of Averroësism. But Dante refuted the philosopher's thought because Averroës mistakenly understood the 'possible intellect' as being *disgiunto da l'anima*[16] (disconnected from the soul), and linked the 'possible intellect' as a single entity to an intellectual concept wholly independent of the body—an angel. Dante the Christian could not have accepted such a line of thought. The Incarnation emphasises the human and the divine united, at one, atoned. Furthermore, as we have seen elsewhere, Free Will is central to the poet's whole understanding of life. The intention to work for the 'possible intellect' must be an act of will, a goal willed by individuals and nations. If the nations of the world are at strife it is because men do not wish the good and the true in their own lives. In this context Dante quotes the first three verses of Psalm 3:

> Why do the heathen rage, and the people imagine a vain thing? The kings of the earth set themselves, and the rulers take counsel together, against the Lord, and against his anointed, saying, let us break their bonds asunder, and cast away their cords from us.

The Roman Empire was seized by force. Dante's 'empire', on the other hand, must be drawn together by peaceful means. The Ancient Empire was however held together through the emperor, and under the rule of Augustus Rome served to bring about 'the fullness of time' when the Saviour was born, who gave himself up to suffer under Roman law, dying to rise again. Rome and the emperor had played a vital role in the history of redemption. Now with the unification of Italy and the other nations, the poet hoped that there would be a new 'fullness of time'. In this, Church and State should be separated, each looking to its own sphere of responsibility. That which is counter to the intent of nature is counter to the will of God. 'Render therefore unto Caesar the things which are Caesar's; and unto God the things that are God's' (Matt. XXII, 21). Note, that for Dante, Christ and not Peter is the rock upon which the Church is built. *Ipse est petra super quam hedificata est Ecclesia.*[17] Had Dante known that in 1440 Lorenzo Valla was to discover that the 'Donation of Constantine' was a bogus document, his censorship of the Papal See would have been all the more severe. Even so, he asserts that the authority of the emperor was derived directly from God. There are two guides leading to blessedness: the emperor, who is the guardian of right-philosophy and whose ideal is to restore the earthly paradise to all peoples; and the pope, who is responsible for the spiritual health of the Church and who is to lead his flock back to the heavenly paradise.

The Paradiso

It is my belief that the Heavens of Dante's cosmology reveal deeper significance when they are related to the Tree of Life as envisaged by the inner tradition known to Jew and Christian. That Dante had access to this ancient teaching there is no doubt in my mind. His grasp of the Tree of Life's symbolism, however, is Christian and could indicate a teaching encountered during his wanderings, for example through a rabbi willing to share his tradition with a gentile or, more likely, a wise monk or priest.

All the Heavens represent contemplative qualities essential to the hastening of the Kingdom. They are fundamental for cleansing the Earthly Paradise (Malkuth) from the consequences displayed in the masque of the Giant and Harlot.[18] The contemplation of the Heavens enables Beatrice (Wisdom and Beatitude) to dwell in the Earthly Paradise, the Kingdom. For Dante we may have either the Dark Wood of thorns and brambles or the trees, flowers and creatures of the Earthly Paradise. The two are the same Wood seen from two different points of view. The Wood sets before us the two ways that are emphasised and laid out in the first psalm of the Psalter. One is where the Giant and Harlot hold sway; the other is where Matelda and Beatrice encounter their lovers.

I will briefly consider the Heavens of the Sun, Mars, Jupiter and Saturn. Once set on the traditional diagram of the Tree of Life it is soon realised that the Eagle of the Heaven of Jupiter (which on one level of interpretation relates to Dante's monarchy[19]) is balanced by the Cross of the Heaven of Mars. Likewise reading the Tree vertically, Mars and Jupiter are 'held' by the Heaven of the Sun; furthermore, both the heavens are fed from above from the Heaven of Saturn, the Heaven of contemplation, meditation and prayer.

Keeping in mind these four Heavens and how they are related on the Tree of Life, it is possible to comprehend Dante's profound understanding of the relationship between Church and State.

First the Heavens of Mars (*Gevurah*, Rigour) and Jupiter (*Hesed*, Mercy) must be grounded in the integrated understanding of love and knowledge of the Heaven of the Sun (*Tiferet*). This Dante is at pains to stress when in Heaven he and Beatrice are surrounded by three circles of fiery souls. Franciscan devotional love is intimately related to the contemplative knowledge of the Dominicans, and vice versa. For example, St Bonaventura is happy to stand next to Joachim of Fiore; so do St John Chrysostom and St Anselm. St Thomas Aquinas stands next to his rival in the earthly life, Sigier of Brabant. St Dionysius the Areopagite, the Neo-Platonist, is quite at peace amidst Aristotelians. All twenty-four souls named dance around the lovers in harmony and without competition or discord. All represent different insights of the truth granted to men and women of faith. The movement of the third circle is seen in the far distance and may represent the harmony granted by the Holy Spirit. Therefore, it is not difficult to conclude that the wise monarch or pope must follow such an example, integrating love and knowledge, harmonising various insights, and not be given to unnecessary repression or inquisition.

Jupiter, the Heaven of the just rulers (*Hesed*), is balanced with Mars, the Heaven of martyrs (*Gevurah*), the Heaven of witness and commitment. There can be no just and merciful state or church without the courage to witness to the truth, as well as the willingness to fight and to die. Fortitude and justice relate to each other at a deep level. A monarch or a pope unwilling to stand up and to be accounted for will never know justice, least of all implement it in their jurisdictions.

All three Heavens (Sun, Mars and Jupiter) are fed by contemplation and meditative prayer and these are symbolised by the Heaven of Saturn (Daath). Right contemplative knowledge enables merciful justice to be known and the courage to bear witness, and to embrace love and knowledge. The teaching is the same for the monarch as it is for the pope. Both are responsible for the happiness and beatitude of their people.

These 'higher' Heavens feed and stabilise the lower three Heavens (the Moon, Mercury and Venus) that are, in the symbolism of the Commedia, tinged by the Earth's shadow. These represent our wavering wills, ambitions and loves.

*

Many read Dante and admire his poetry, few share his politics or religion, and yet his work is 'one of the few monuments of human achievement'.[20] This is because Dante speaks from the perennial wisdom and the archetypal worlds. The ideas and concepts with which his works brim come from an awakening of love and the courage to follow that love wherever it took him, from the lowest hell to the highest heaven. Fundamental, therefore, is the reader's own awakening, his acknowledgement of his encounter with the 'burning bush', and the metanoia thereby implied. Dante would call all his readers to know the nobility of the soul; that is, a soul vibrant in love and desire for knowledge, inspired by the feminine mysteries. Pope, monarch, laity, all are called to stand before the Theotokos, the Mother of God, she whose example teaches her lovers how they too may bring the mystery of the Incarnation into this world and so hasten the coming of the Kingdom.

Bibliography

—Dante Alighieri, La Vita Nuova di Dante Alighieri, con il commento di Tommaso Casini (Florence, 1951).
—Il Convivio (Milan, 1977).

—The Convivio of Dante Alighieri, translated and with notes by Philip H. Wicksteed (London, 1903).

—De Vulgari Eloquentia : Dante's Book of Exile, translated with comments by Marianne Shapiro (Lincoln and London, 1990).

—A translation of Dante's Eleven Letters, with notes and historical comments by Charles Sterrett Latham (Boston and New York, 1892).

—Monarchy and three political letters, translated with an introduction by Donald Nicholl (London, 1954).

—La Divina Commedia, testo critico della Società Dantesca Italiana (Milan, 1965).

*

—Peter Armour, Dante's Grifffin and the History of the World. A Study of the Earthly Paradise (Purgatorio, cantos XXIX–XXXIII) (Oxford, 1989).

—A. P. d'Entrèves, Dante as a Political Thinker (Oxford, 1952).

—Etienne Gilson, Dante and Philosophy (New York and London, 1949).

—Robert Hollander, Dante: A Life in Works (New Haven and London, 2001).

—Charles Williams, The Figure of Beatrice. A Study in Dante (London, 1943).

NOTES

1. Dante understood his experience as his transfiguration, the significance of which he only grasped towards the end of his life when he came to write the Paradiso. See Vita Nuova XIV.

2. Vita Nuova XII. 5.

3. Vita Nuova XII. 3.

4. Vita Nuova XII. 4.

5. Paradiso XV. 97, 99.

6. Convivio IV. iv. 8.

7. Convivio IV.

8. Boniface had intrigued in the poet's expulsion from Florence and was an enemy of the Franciscan Spirituals.

9. Clement sided with Philip IV of France. Philip opposed the recognition of Dante's hero Henry IV of Luxembourg as Emperor and persecuted the Knights Templar. Clement carried even further Boniface's theocratic ideas, asserting papal authority over the Empire.

10. This theme is admirably illustrated by Botticelli's Mystic Nativity in the National

Gallery, London. Botticelli turned later in his career from the Neoplatonism of the Medici to an apocalyptic Christianity, under the influence of Savonarola and a revaluation of Dante's texts.

11. See *De Monarchia* I. xii.6 and *Paradiso* V. 19–24.

12. 2 Sam. 6:3.

13. *Purgatorio* X. 57 and *Epistle* XI. 9–12.

14. The imagery of the Ark is explored to the full in the concluding cantos of the *Purgatorio*, in which the symbolism of the chariot, at first occupied by Beatrice and then by the Giant and Harlot, is clearly also the Ark.

15. These are the root sins of the abyss in the *Inferno*.

16. *Purgatorio* XXV. 63–66.

17. *De Monarchia* III. 7.

18. *Purgatorio* XXXIII.

19. On another level of interpretation, it is the eagle of St John, the eagle of visionary knowledge. The pupil of the eagle's eye is David—the psalmist.

20. Robert Hollander, *Dante: a Life in Works* (New Haven and London, 2001) 179.

JOSEPH MILNE
SHAKESPEARE & DIVINE KINGSHIP

Nothing is more obvious than that Shakespeare's works are the fruits of poetic vision. That is to say, they mirror reality according to poetic vision in order that we should apprehend for a moment something of that vision. Nothing is more obvious than this, and yet it is the one thing that is most often forgotten or even entirely overlooked in interpretations of Shakespeare. If we listen to Shakespeare attentively our perception is raised to another level and our ordinary apprehension transformed from a fragmented grasping of mundane things to a sense of universality and universal presence. Poetic vision is concerned with the divine powers within and without that animate and move all things and which, all taken together, disclose the divine mystery that is the universe. This divine mystery of the universe is not unmasked or explained through poetic vision, and therefore rendered no longer a mystery, but rather in some way made present in its mystery. It is therefore quite wrong to seek some doctrine in Shakespeare which explains his work to non-poetic vision. On the contrary, it is our vision that must be transformed into poetic vision, rather than poetic vision degraded into mundane vision. This transformative power is the mark of all true art, even the very humblest work of true art. And that which is not true art is known by its lack of this transformative power.

It is very odd, if you think about it, that poetic vision is so often interpreted in terms of non-poetic vision. We do not interpret mathematics in terms of non-mathematics, or history in terms of non-history, or grammar in terms of non-grammar, yet all too often poetry in interpreted in terms of the non-poetic—in terms of historical context, social conditions, psychology, religious doctrine and so on. All these approaches miss the point, not to mention the simple fact that none of these things are themselves clear knowledge of the truth of reality. On the other hand perhaps they are understandable in our times when it is generally believed that the only kind of knowledge is analytical and measurable, when everything is sought to be understood in concrete terms and when theory replaces direct perception of reality itself as it reveals itself. Poetic vision is not an interpretation of reality but rather a glimpse of what reality utters out of itself, a setting down of what the mystery wills to communicate of itself. Hence, like prophetic vision, it is inspired, revealed from above, manifested in terms of itself. Thus, for the poet's eye everything visible is communicating something invisible and thus disclosing how every material appearance bears the infinite mystery within itself. And this mystery cannot be made into a non-mystery. Rather, poetic vision remains an abiding with the mystery, and the transformative power of true art brings about in the listener a similar abiding with the mystery. Everything that is, so to speak, is whispering the same mystery, and it is to this that the poetic vision bears witness. The world is presencing the infinite mystery, and in this sense the world means itself. All objective or subjective theory or explanation of the world disregards this simple fact, dismisses the divine presence manifesting itself.

Poetic vision, then, is attuned to this disclosing power that belongs to reality itself. So when the poet speaks of the rose or the lily, of the sun or the stars, the forest or the cloud, of the city or the gods, he does not mean some other thing by these things but rather what these things truly are in their own natures and what they speak in their own disclosing.

> Sit, Jessica. Look how the floor of heaven
> Is thick inlaid with patines of bright gold;
> There's not the smallest orb which thou behold'st
> But in his motion like an angel sings,
> Still quiring to the young-ey'd cherubins;
> Such harmony is in immortal souls,
> But whilst this muddy vesture of decay

Doth grossly close it in, we cannot hear it.

(*Merchant of Venice*, V.i)

Lorenzo and Jessica may not quite hear that celestial harmony, yet even so, as lovers, they attend to it, and even as they attend to it the musicians enter and through the art of music they imitate and bear witness to that celestial harmony. Thus the celestial harmony does become audible through the mediation of art. At a single stroke Shakespeare has here presented all we have just observed about poetic vision. But he has added something else which is pertinent to our theme of divine kingship: there is a correspondence between the celestial music of the heavens and the harmony in immortal souls. That is to say, there is a correlation between the nature of the soul and the divine motions of the heavens. But while the immortal soul is closed within the mortal it knows neither the harmony within nor without—and yet that harmony may be mediated through the art of music and so bring the immortal soul into recollection of itself and into harmony with the cosmic harmony.

This recollection of the soul to itself and its attunement to the celestial harmony is just one way in which Shakespeare shows us the nature of divine sovereignty. The crown mediates between the immortal and the mortal, or between the eternal and the temporal, and through this mediation brings about a correspondence or alignment between the human and the cosmic order. This alignment between the inner order of the human soul and the universal order of the cosmos is a key to understanding Shakespeare's presentation of reality and in particular of divine kingship. We may suggest that this is the very essence of drama. In each of Shakespeare's plays we are presented with an entire world in which every action and every event is connected not only through the characters but through the cosmos itself. We enter a living cosmos ordered according to eternal laws which play themselves out in the lands and kingdoms of the world as well as within the human souls, a world in which all things move according to divine providence or destiny, in which every human action or decision becomes part of the cosmic fabric and has universal consequences or repercussions. Even though the plays draw us into this cosmic order, we as a modern audience need to lay aside most of the prevailing notions of human nature and of the world in order to witness their coherence. Modern psychological notions are foreign here, for Shakespeare's characters do not act or move according to modern psychological motivations or unconscious drives. Shakespeare's characters are not hidden or alienated from themselves as modern man is conceived to be. Likewise all modern notions of the physics of the universe are foreign here, for Shakespeare's cosmos is not an inert mechanism but rather a living realm which unfolds and moves according to divine ends that touch the human soul directly. Human and cosmic destiny are bound together, and the unity of these two is what Shakespeare calls 'nature'.

This relation between the human soul and the cosmos is the pattern of the relation of subject to the crown. Thus in Shakespeare a kingdom presents to us all the relations that move and order the heavens and the earth in the hierarchy of the human society, and the divine destiny that shapes the ends of the cosmos descends, so to speak, and is gathered into the crown. And within this structure of the state the divine order descends a further step to the individual who likewise is, so to speak, a little kingdom within the greater kingdom of the state, just as the state is a little kingdom within the cosmic state. In this way providence or divine destiny manifests on three levels or three different scales. Thus to follow cosmic law, the law of the crown and the law of the individual soul all come to the same thing. To put that another way, to follow the call of cosmic destiny, the will of the crown and individual human conscience are three forms of the same ground of action. Within this structure everything reveals its proper end or fulfilment. Something of this may be illustrated in the meeting of Macbeth and Banquo with Duncan before Macbeth goes astray:

> Macbeth The service and the loyalty I owe,
>   In doing it, pays itself. Your Highness' part

Is to receive our duties, and our duties
Are to your throne and state, children and servants,
Which do but what they should, by doing everything
Safe toward your love and honour.

Duncan Welcome hither.
I have begun to plant thee, and will labour
To make thee full of growing. Noble Banquo,
That hast no less deserved, nor must be known
No less to have done so; let me infold thee
And hold thee to my heart.

Banquo There if I grow,
The harvest is your own.

(*Macbeth*, I.iv)

Mark the words of Macbeth, our duties do what they should 'by doing everything safe towards your love and honour'. The words 'duty', 'love' and 'honour' are seminal words in Shakespeare and represent the authentic ground of all human action that brings the celestial order and the human order together. These three are the bonds which hold all things together, and because that is so it is the breaking of these bonds that leads to tragedy and destruction. Whatever 'evil' may be it always involves breaking these bonds. Mark also the response of Duncan: 'I have begun to plant thee, and will labour to make thee full of growing'. Here Macbeth's true destiny and calling is signified, a destiny which we know, of course, that he fails to fulfil by choosing to take all that belongs to true kingship to himself for his own, and thus inverting the cosmic order, the central theme of this play. Banquo's response is the true response: 'There if I grow, the harvest is your own'.

These few words of Duncan indicate the true meaning of kingship as Shakespeare presents it. The true king nurtures and brings to fruition the true destinies of the individuals that comprise the kingdom, and this nurturing is possible because the crown mediates divine providence or grace. Thus kingship is a calling and the election of a king is itself a matter of destiny or descent and not personal human will. We are given an extraordinary glimpse of the grace which may pass through a true king later in *Macbeth* when Macduff comes in despair to seek the help of England. Here Malcolm, later to be crowned the rightful king of Scotland, speaks to Macduff of the strange disease which ordinary medicine cannot heal:

> *Malcolm* 'Tis call'd the evil:
> A most miraculous work in this good King,
> Which often, since my here-remain in England,
> I have seen him do. How he solicits heaven,
> Himself best knows; but strangely-visited people,
> All swol'n and ulcerous, pitiful to the eye,
> The mere despair of surgery, he cures,
> Hanging a golden stamp about their necks
> Put on with holy prayers; and 'tis spoken,
> To the succeeding royalty he leaves
> The healing benediction. With this strange virtue
> He hath a heavenly gift of prophecy,
> And sundry blessings hang about his throne
> That speak him full of grace.
>
> (*Macbeth*, IV.iii)

In these few lines the qualities of monarch, prophet and saint are merged into one, and a power to solicit heaven and cure 'strangely visited people' of 'the evil' makes him also a divine healer of maladies the 'despair of surgery', that is, ordinary human medicine. The 'sundry blessings' about his thrown 'that speak him full of grace' indicate the source of his divine powers, for grace is the mark of the true king as mediator of the divine power of goodness. Within the context of this play this revelation of divine kingship is highly significant. Macduff has come to England in despair of Scotland, having lost all, and is here being tested by Malcolm to see where his allegiancies lie—either with tyranny or divinity. The rule of Macbeth in Scotland represents the exact opposite of true

kingship. Through the usurpation of the crown for his own ambitions Macbeth has ushered in a reign of darkness and destruction
where even the regular courses of nature are disrupted and where
fear reigns where love should reign. Thus the sudden news of divine
kingship enters the play at its decisive moment. When all seems
utterly lost, suddenly all may be reversed and true kingship may be
restored to Scotland. It is rather a shame that this scene is often
omitted in performances of the play on the grounds that it has no
action, while in fact it is the turning-point of the whole drama
if looked at from the cosmic point of view, that is, in terms of
the relationship of heaven and earth as mediated through kingship.
If the play is interpreted merely in terms of the psychology or
character of Macbeth, then this subtler dimension of grace and true
majesty is missed and may even seem irrelevant. For Shakespeare
the destinies of peoples or kingdoms are not determined by traits of
human character but rather by the way in which the protagonists
are oriented to the invisible powers of the heavens, and whether
they align themselves with them or defy them. By way of testing
Macduff's true motives for coming to England, Malcolm feigns to
lack all the kingly qualities:

> Malcolm   But I have none. The king-becoming graces,
>   As justice, verity, temperance, stableness,
>   Bounty, perseverance, mercy, lowliness,
>   Devotion, patience, courage, fortitude,
>   I have no relish of them, but abound
>   In the division of each several crime,
>   Acting it many ways. Nay, had I power, I should
>   Pour the sweet milk of concord into hell,
>   Uproar the universal peace, confound
>   All unity on earth.
>
> (Macbeth, IV.iii)

We observe that the overthrow of all the kingly virtues brings
universal division and discord:

... had I power, I should
Pour the sweet milk of concord into hell,
Uproar the universal peace, confound
All unity on earth.

This is the true consequence of tyranny in Shakespeare's cosmology. It is not merely a matter of whether the king is good or bad in his own character simply as an individual, but whether his qualities bring peace and concord throughout the realm or 'confound all unity'. To break the concord between heaven and earth brings chaos, strife and division in all human affairs, and through this division cuts human life off from attaining its natural ends. The higher potentialities of the individual can be realized only in a peaceful kingdom where all the natural human institutions work in harmony.

In Macbeth this chaos and division is writ large and commences even at the moment he murders Duncan in his sleep. In a play such as *Hamlet*, however, the ensuing chaos is more hidden. Here Claudius, like Macbeth, has murdered the true king in his sleep, but unlike Macbeth, he attempts to act as a good king. While Macbeth is moved to seize power entirely for his own satisfaction, Claudius desires to assume the divine attributes of kingship. He desires to be loved as a true king, and for some time this appears to work for him. He has the love of the Queen and the loyalty of the entire court, and especially of Polonius who personifies devotion and fidelity. He has taken all precautions against the unruly Fortinbrass who threatens the kingdom. On the surface all seems well. Yet it is a feigned kingship. Shakespeare here presents us with a very curious and fascinating situation. Claudius attempts to act as a good king. He desires peace and concord. The first time we see him he speaks and acts with grace and largesse. It is therefore quite wrong when actors play him as devious and false in the first act. He is attempting to assume true kingly qualities. He would even win the love of Hamlet. Unlike Macbeth, he has no further evil intentions, not even to disinherit Hamlet from the succession. He has, so to speak, done one thing wrong but would now do all things right.

Yet it is only when we see the meaning of kingship as cosmic mediator that we know this cannot work. Claudius' good intentions are not enough, not because they are insincere but because they are founded upon breaking the original divine election of kingship. He has taken the throne of Denmark by breaking the harmony between heaven and earth, and it is that severing of the divine order that will play out its consequences. To this Claudius is entirely blind. He attempts to accomplish through pragmatic intelligence, which he has in abundance, what can only be accomplished through divine virtue. He is oblivious of the laws that actually rule kingdoms and events. He would rule through human ingenuity alone. Here Shakespeare is showing us an extraordinary thing: that the affairs of state, and therefore of human life as such, cannot be conducted to their true ends by means of good intentions and pragmatic intelligence alone. Thus, despite all appearances of good order, a strange darkness hovers beneath, manifesting first in the confusion of the guards at the opening of the play, then in the fumblings of Polonius and in the immovable black mood that possesses Hamlet. Here Polonius is a most interesting character. He is usually played as a verbose fool, but his verbosity and rhetorical embroidery are not the result of foolishness or indulgence, but rather of absolute faithfulness taken out of its ground. Polonius can only be a true servant under the grace of a true king. Thus in Polonius we have true devotion and absolute loyalty juxtaposed to a false embodiment of divine kingship in Claudius. That which Polonius is born to serve, and under which alone he can properly function, has been removed and so he cannot act true to himself. Polonius personifies the devotion and loyalty of the whole of Denmark to the crown, and it is the function of the crown to bring that devotion and loyalty to fruition, as we saw earlier in the words of Duncan in *Macbeth*. Therefore it is the deficiency of Claudius that leads all Polonius's good will astray, and Polonius finally to his death. Polonius is placed in the false position of serving a false good.

Love and loyalty cannot be built on a false foundation. That is the law that this play shows us. Gradually all the bonds of love in this play go astray. The relation between Polonius and his son Laertes is marred by mistrust creeping in; Laertes questions the truth of Hamlet's love for his sister Ophelia; the darkness that falls upon Hamlet himself leads him to deny that love. The only constant loyalty and love in the play that endures is that between Hamlet and Horatio—but Horatio is not of Denmark and therefore outside the fate that befalls Denmark. Of all this Claudius remains oblivious. He has the position and office of kingship, but not the divine vision and graces that belong to that office, and so his kingship can lead only to the gradual disintegration and final fall of Denmark. This is a cosmic law as Shakespeare presents the inner meaning of kingship to us in his plays. A kingdom cannot become concordant and fruitful merely by playing politics with good intentions, or by pragmatic diplomacy, as Claudius attempts to do. Human law and human action must be grounded in heavenly law and correspond with divine action. Once the link between the human and the divine is broken even the best of human intentions go astray and fail in their ends. That is the seminal lesson of this play. Therefore to attempt to understand *Hamlet* simply on the human level, or in terms of the psychologies or passions of the characters, is to miss the point. Indeed, the play remains incoherent approached in that limited way. Shakespeare is not concerned to show us the inner workings of the human psyche but rather the relations that exist in the fabric of things between the earthly and the divine, or between the immortal soul and the celestial harmony. Therefore the question in this play is not whether Hamlet should avenge his father's murder, even though on the human level that seems to be the question, but rather how may he restore the concord between the state of Denmark and the heavenly order.

*

From these observations of kingship in some of Shakespeare's plays it is worth asking ourselves what kind of vision of reality they present to us. It seems to me that there are three fundamental things. First, that there is a relation between the order of the state or kingdom and the cosmic order. Second, there is a relation between the inner order of the individual soul and the way in which the world is apprehended. And third, that the inner intention of any action produces lawful consequences. These form the very fabric of the plays. They are not notions imposed upon them from outside. This is how the world appears to poetic vision. Poetic vision encompasses the whole of reality at a glance and brings to light the correspondences and relations between all the different levels of reality, the inner and the outer, the universal and the particular, cause and effect, origin and destiny, past and future. Although scholars of Shakespeare find references to social and political concerns and events of his time, these are merely incidental. One does not find the meaning of his plays through study of literal history any more than through study of the texts Shakespeare used as his sources. On the contrary, all the materials Shakespeare takes up, from whatever source, are shaped and adapted to his larger poetic vision. The world is the vocabulary of the poet, the letters of the poetic alphabet so to speak, but not the meaning. Shakespeare is not commenting on the world, but reflecting its nature.

To the modern ear it may sound strange to speak of poetic vision in this way, but this is because the poets have largely forgotten their function within society, and instead of embodying universal vision have become preoccupied with the superficialities of the everyday and the merely personal. True poetry is grounded in the soil of civilisation, and this means the true poet locates his or her voice in the essence of culture and the speech of mankind, on a plane above the issues of the times and therefore above the social and political preoccupations of the times. In this respect the poet complements the prophet and the philosopher, the prophet speaking to the conscience, the philosopher to the reason and the poet to the heart, the three ways of apprehending the True, the Good and the Beautiful in Platonic terms.

The soil of Western civilisation is a blend of the Christian and

Classical Greek visions of reality, and these clearly lie at the heart of Shakespeare's representations of the qualities of kingship. The Renaissance, as we know, was a new convergence and synthesis of these. From Plato and Plotinus comes the Greek vision of the cosmic harmony, the hierarchical emanation from the One to the many, from which comes the central conception in English Common Law of natural justice, that is, the disposition of nature to justice in all its parts. From the Christian vision of Divine Grace comes the understanding that all things are directed to the good through Divine Love. The philosophical vision comes from the discernment of nature through reason, and the religious vision through the gift of divine revelation. Thus we find Blackstone, the great seventeenth-century commentator on English Common Law, says that all law derives from the power, wisdom and goodness of the Creator, and because it derives from these three together the Creator

> has been pleased so to contrive the constitution and frame of humanity, that we should want no other prompter to inquire after and pursue the rule of right, but only our own self-love, that universal principle of action. For he has so intimately connected, so inseparably interwoven the laws of eternal justice with the happiness of each individual, that the latter cannot be attained but by observing the former; and, if the former be punctually obeyed, it cannot but induce the latter.

The natural desire in every human being for happiness, springing from the soul's love of its own being which it has received as a gift from the Creator, finds its fulfilment only through attending to the laws of eternal justice, and therefore through desiring the mutual good of every being. As Thomas Aquinas says, 'every being seeks its own good'. This seeking the good is universal. No being desires evil for itself. Neither does the universe taken as whole seek anything other than universal good. Here is the natural basis of the universal harmony between all beings and all laws.

This conception of the basis of law is a blend of Greek and Christian vision. From the Greek philosophers, as we have said, comes the understanding of cosmic order, the celestial harmony that Lorenzo bids Jessica to contemplate. These are the rational courses of the heavens Plato asks us in the *Timaeus* to conform the courses of our own intelligence to. Thus we may say that the Greek vision is based upon the raising of the mind to mystical contemplation of the being of the universe, and through that contemplation bring about a correspondence between the divine cosmic order and the inner order of the immortal soul. From this essence of Greek philosophy we derive Western ontology, the philosophy of being or metaphysics.

The Christian revelation, on the other hand, bids us to right action, and right action extends beyond justice or natural law to action from grace or *caritas*, that is, action from divine love. Here we find a marked and most interesting difference between Greek drama and Shakespeare. In Greek drama all human struggles and dilemmas spring from the relation of mortals to Fate, a view which finds later expression in the Stoic philosophers. But in Shakespeare there is another realm above this realm of Fate, the realm of divine Grace, the realm of infinite goodness that raises human destiny above Fate and into providential care. In Greek thought providence is justice, in Christian thought it is Grace. Thus in Shakespeare, with this profoundly Christian element, the struggles, desires and dilemmas of human existence are centred upon the human decision either to follow the universal good or to fall, through denial of that universal good, under the powers of dissolution and destruction. For Shakespeare the will is central, the power to make ultimate decisions, and in this respect his view of human nature is existential rather than ontological. While in Greek drama the ultimate outcome is determined by the gods or Fate, virtually regardless of human intention, in Shakespeare the outcome of drama is the lawful consequence of human intention and decision. Both views are equally lawful. The Greek vision shows that mortals cannot defy the will of the gods, while the Shakespearean vision shows that man cannot escape the consequences of his own intentions and actions. For Shakespeare each individual, and likewise each state or kingdom, is responsible for their own destiny, but within the law of divine dispensation or providence. Thus we may say that the 'self-love' implanted in the human heart by the Creator may rise up and extend itself to encompass and unite with the will of God, and through this union become the mediator of divine Grace on earth. This is the essence of Shakespeare's vision of kingship. It is also the essence of his vision of the State. Through the crown descends the grace that nurtures and makes all members of the State grow, and through the duties of the members of the State to the crown through love and honour each receives their due in the delight of performing their duties and following their natural callings in service towards the whole. In this way love, justice, loyalty and duty within the State bring the State into harmony with the celestial or cosmic harmony.

Here, all that may be said of kingship in Shakespeare may be said of the human individual. The kingdom, the king and the individual are one and the same. This correspondence has its roots once again in Plato who, in the Republic, draws exact analogies between the different kinds of states, aristocracy, timocracy, democracy and tyranny, and the different human types. But Shakespeare has fused this with the medieval vision of the integration of the individual with the State, which was then the basis of education. The ideal medieval man was one who could act on behalf of the whole society. This is the basis of the social hierarchy. It is not a hierarchy of the powerful over the powerless, but of greater goodness and service, of capacity to act above mere personal self-interest. All this is founded on the understanding that there is a relation between the essence of the human soul and the cosmic order or, to put that in Christian terms, that man is made in the image of God and can therefore act in godlike ways by conforming himself to his own true essence. Yet when Shakespeare shows his kings acting from that essence he shows it as the mediation of divine grace, as the supernatural acting through the human individual, because, in a sense, the individual has become universal and acts from the ground of the divine will. In medieval terms this is to act from the Angelic Mind, the highest apex of the soul which resides closest to the mind of God and which apprehends universals.

It would be wrong, however, to suppose that Shakespeare derives his representation of kingship from philosophical ideas or religious doctrines, let alone from political theories or social issues. That would be to misunderstand poetic vision, and Shakespeare is above all a poet. Poetic vision is itself a manner of apprehending reality and bodying it forth through the word in such a way that essence is made tangible to us, given 'local habitation and a name'. It is an apprehension that grasps the whole, from heaven to earth, invisible and visible, inner and outer, and makes manifest the mysterious laws that govern and unite all things. It is true that the great philosophers and mystics have this universal vision too, but in a different manner and addressing us differently. The poetic vision has the capacity to address us at all levels at once, and thus it speaks from the essence of our culture, the essence of language, to that same essence in us. The poet speaks to us as universal beings, as immortal souls and as members of the cosmic drama, and in that sense may hold up a mirror in which we can see ourselves and our world, showing us what we are and where we are within the context of eternity and the present at a single stroke. Thus, in the poet's eye, all the things of nature, of society, of institutions and of civilisation itself, disclose a divine meaning once their harmony has been seen, and the power that brings all these things into being is Grace. All these things converge in kingship or the crown, but here in the act of pure service to the whole.

GREVEL LINDOP

THE WHEEL-TURNING MONARCH:
AN IDEAL OF KINGSHIP IN EARLY BUDDHISM

The teachings concerning the Cakkavatti Raja or Wheel-Turning
King are very little known amongst Buddhists, especially in the
Western world. Partly this may be because this mythology offers
a role-model for the lay person, the 'householder', as opposed to the
monk or ascetic—the 'homeless one'. It is thus perhaps less likely to
seem of central importance to the monastic teachers and scholars,
the sangha, who have traditionally been the transmitters of Buddhist
texts across the centuries. At the same time, as a body of teaching
couched in distinctly mythological terms, it has not appealed
greatly to the western teachers who over the past century or so have
taken an interest in Buddhism as a supposedly 'rational' or
'scientific' religion. The teachings about the Wheel-Turning King
are likely to appear to such people as mythological encrustations
overlaying the pure and supposedly simple body of the Buddha's
authentic doctrine.

In fact this perspective is very far from having any sound basis.
The suttas containing the main traditions on this theme are part of
the Digha Nikaya or collection of the Buddha's 'long discourses' in
the Pali canon, the Buddhist scriptures of the southern Buddhist or
Theravada countries of Thailand, Sri Lanka, Vietnam, Laos, Burma
and Cambodia. These are among the oldest of the Buddhist texts;
and the material shows no signs of being less authentic than any
other part of the Buddha's teachings. Moreover, aspects and details
of the myth of the Wheel-Turning King are woven into countless
other parts of Buddhist culture, ranging from the legends about the
Buddha's birth recounted in the Southern Buddhist countries to
details of innumerable Tibetan texts and practices—a fact which
shows that the myth travelled at an early date to North India and

the regions, such as Tibet itself, which derived their transmission of Buddhism from that area. The word 'myth' is, of course, used here not to indicate any lack of truth or authenticity, but rather the reverse. The Buddhist teachings about the ideal king and his tasks are a fundamental part of Buddhist cosmology and contain, in poetic and visionary form, profound wisdom about the nature and purpose of human life and how it can best be lived.

Perhaps the best way for us to enter this particular mythical realm is to recall a familiar legend about the early infancy of the Prince Siddhattha, who would later become known (after his Enlightenment) as the Lord Buddha. Soon after the prince's birth, it is said that a number of Brahmin soothsayers were summoned to look at him and make predictions about his future career. Most of the Brahmins reported that from certain signs on the child's body, they could tell that only two future possibilities lay open to him. Either he would be a wheel-turning king, one who would rule justly over the whole known world, or else he would become a Buddha, a fully enlightened spiritual teacher. In fact just one of the soothsayers, the young Kondañña, predicted with certainty that the child would become a Buddha—there were no two ways about it. But the others thought that they could see either possibility.

What is happening here is that the Brahmins are recognising the child as a *Mahapurisa*—a 'Great Man'—by the qualities of his body. These qualities or marks, of which there are thirty-two in all, are set out in another early Buddhist text—the *Lakkhana Sutta*—the 'Discourse on the Marks or Signs'. Some of these signs are matters of proportion or beauty: for example, we are told that his proportions are like the sphere of the banyan tree—'as long as his body, so far is the span of his arms; as far as the span of his arms, so long is the body'; that he has very blue eyes, and that his voice is like 'the voice of Brahma, resembling the song of a *karavika* bird'.[1] Other signs seem to be perceptible only to some form of psychic vision, perhaps thought of as similar to that attributed to people who can perceive the human aura: for instance, that he has wheels, complete with a thousand spokes, on his hands and feet—a feature which is sometimes represented on statues of the Buddha in various parts of the world, where the palms of the hands or the soles of the feet may be delicately engraved with the wheel-symbols. These marks, according to the Lakkhana Sutta, are the result of the excellent actions the Mahapurisa or Great Man has performed in previous lifetimes; and each indicates a specific quality, depending on whether he becomes a king or a Buddha.

Thus the voice like Brahma's, resembling the song of the karavika bird, is the result of his having, in previous lives, abstained from harsh speech, and practised instead speech which is 'gentle, pleasant to hear, affectionate, reaching to the heart, courteous, dear to the people, pleasing to the people.' It indicates that if he now becomes a king, his words will be heeded by 'Brahmins and house-holders, townsfolk and countryfolk, treasurers and ministers, royal guards, doorkeepers, courtiers, councillors, princes, nobles and noble youths'.[2] On the other hand if he becomes a Buddha, an Awakened One, his words will be heeded by monks and nuns, male and female lay disciples, gods, humans, asuras, nagas (dragons) and gandhabas (fairies or nature-spirits). And so on.

Since Prince Siddhattha goes on, despite his father's best endeavours, to become a Buddha, the other alternative—that a child with such a body may grow up to be a wheel-turning monarch—is usually dropped without further discussion. But it is worth noting that this myth of the bodily marks indicates that the Buddha and the wheel-turning king are, from one point of view, two of a kind. Both are Mahapurisa—Great Men with a special destiny, one sacred and the other secular.

The central myth of the Wheel-Turning King is set out in detail principally in two suttas of the Pali canon, the Mahasudassanasutta and the Cakavattisihanadasutta. The Mahasudassanasutta, takes us, significantly, to the other end of the Buddha's life, for in this text he is in old age, with his companion the Venerable Ananda, at Kusinara, shortly before the Buddha's final passing away. Ananda is made anxious by the thought that his Master may pass away in this 'miserable little town of wattle and daub' and urges him to travel on to somewhere more fitting, such as the holy city of Benares. The Buddha replies with a story. Once upon a time, aeons ago, he tells Ananda, what is now this insignificant small town of Kusinara was a great city, then called Kusavati, the capital city of King Mahasudassana, a wheel-turning monarch, 'a rightful and righteous king, who had conquered the land in four directions and ensured the security of his realm.'[3]

We move now into the brilliant and magical visualisation which is such an important feature of these texts.

The royal city of Kusavati [the Buddha continues] was surrounded by seven encircling walls. One was of gold, one silver, one beryl, one crystal, one ruby, one emeralds, and one of all kinds of gems.

And the gates of Kusavati were of four colours: one gold, one silver, one beryl, one crystal. And before each gate were set seven pillars . . . One was of gold, one of silver, one beryl, one crystal, one ruby, one of emeralds, and one of all sorts of gems.[4]

The picture of this cosmic mandala-like city becomes still more intricate as he proceeds:

Kusavati was surrounded by seven rows of palm trees of the same materials. The gold trees had gold trunks with silver leaves and fruit; the silver trees had silver trunks with gold leaves and fruit; the beryl trees had beryl trunks with crystal leaves and fruit; the crystal trees had crystal trunks with beryl leaves and fruit[5]

. . . and so on and so forth. And to round it all off, to complete the picture, as it were, we are told that 'The sound of the leaves stirred by the wind was lovely, delightful, sweet and intoxicating, just like that of the five kinds of musical instruments played in concert by well-trained and skilful players.' And, according to a controversial translation of a difficult passage by Rhys Davids, which Maurice Walshe regards as absurd but which is surely rather attractive, 'whoever . . . in the royal city of Kusavati were at that time gamblers, drunkards, and given to drink, they used to dance round together to the sound of those palms when shaken by the wind.'[6]

This scene-setting is of great importance. One of its functions is to induce in the reader an enormously complex imaginative vision which is harmonious but also which tends to escape the limits of the mind's conceptions. The intricate, almost mathematical per-mutations of colours and jewels create an impression of infinite varied repetition, as if we were inside an enormous hall of mirrors which not only reflected images over and over again in all direc-tions, but constantly changed and substituted the details of colour and pattern. For the city is, of course, on one level a model of the cosmos; and on another, a symbol for the endless perspectives, repe-titions and transformations of the life of conscious beings in a cosmos where beings are reincarnated in life after life, constantly echoing and constantly changing the patterns already established.

Now, within this city, we are told, lived King Mahasudassana. And King Mahasudassana possessed seven treasures, of which the most important was the wheel-treasure. How did he acquire it? Well, once, on a full-moon day (a day of religious observance in Buddhist countries), when the King had washed his head and gone up to the terrace on top of his palace to observe the fast-day, 'the divine wheel-treasure appeared to him, thousand-spoked, com-plete with felloe, hub and all appurtenances.' It seems that we are to imagine this great and beautiful wheel appearing in the heavens before him. The King thinks to himself, 'I have heard that when a duly-anointed . . . king sees such a wheel on a fast-day . . . he will become a wheel-turning monarch.' And he makes the aspiration, 'May I become such a monarch.' He rises up, covers one shoulder with his robe, and taking a golden vessel in his hand, with his right hand sprinkles water over the wheel, saying 'May the noble wheel-treasure turn, may the noble wheel-treasure conquer.'[7] The wheel then turns to the east, to the south, to the west and to the north, in each direction plunging into the sea ands then emerging to continue its journey. The King follows the wheel in each direction, we are told, with his army; and in each direction, as he follows the wheel, the lesser kings whom he meets welcome him and offer him submission. Accepting their submission, the King replies: 'Do not take life. Do not take what is not given. Do not commit sexual misconduct. Do not tell lies. Do not take intoxicants.' In other words, he teaches them the five precepts or rules of training which are the foundations of Buddhist morality. He adds a phrase of which the translation is uncertain but which Rhys Davids translates as 'Ye shall eat as ye have eaten'[8]—apparently implying that the King wishes his new subjects to keep their social customs and traditions unchanged, and that unlike most conquerors he has no wish to impose alien customs upon them. And after this the wheel returns to the palace and remains there, as if to adorn it.

We now understand why the King is called a wheel-turning monarch. He is a king who has had a vision of the sacred wheel of Dhamma, and who rules by its virtue, basing his rule on a humane and generous reminding of his subjects that their first duty, to him and to themselves, is to live wisely and well. But what is the wheel-treasure? In one sense, clearly, it is the sun; we are being reminded of the ancient associations, present in all cultures, between kingship and the sun. But it has many more meanings. It forms another link between the ideas of king and Buddha, since the Buddha's teaching is frequently symbolised as a wheel, and the Buddha's first sermon is always known as the 'Turning of the Wheel of Dhamma'. Both Buddha and King are thus Turners of Wheels. And we recall in this connection that one mark of the Great Man is that he has wheels on his hands and feet—wheels with a thousands spokes with the nave and the tyre complete, exactly like the one seen by the King. But the wheel also has an inner or psychological significance. We remember that the wheel appeared on a fast-day, when the King had gone up to the upper terrace of his palace to observe the fast. The implication is unavoidable that the wheel, appearing to him at just that point, is also an internal experience; it may be thought of as appearing not in the external heavens but rather in the King's own mind, as a form of the mental image or *nimitta*—a light, a disc of colour, or other mandala-like focal image, which is said to arise in the mind of one practising tranquil meditation when he comes to the threshold of a fully-integrated contemplative state. From this point of view the wheel is the symbol of the King's purification of his own mind, of his inner balance, calm and benevolence. A conquest of the world naturally follows, not a military conquest but a supremacy based simply on goodness, good will, and spiritual radiance which renders military conquest irrelevant.

But the King has seven treasures in all. The wheel is only one of them. What are the others? Well, they are the elephant treasure, the horse-treasure, the jewel-treasure, the woman-treasure, the house-holder-treasure, and the counsellor-treasure. All have special properties. The elephant-treasure (which is called *Uposatha*, the word for one of the lunar quarter-days: recall the day on which the wheel first appeared) can fly through the air and carry the King from sea to sea between sunrise and breakfast time. The horse-treasure likewise flies through the air and performs similar feats to the elephant. The jewel-treasure is a perfect beryl, so fine that it radiates light for a whole league around, and the King's army can practise manoeuvres by night simply by its light. The woman-treasure is the queen: she has divine beauty; 'the touch of the skin of the woman-treasure was like cotton or silk, and her limbs were cool when it was hot, and warm when it was cold. Her body smelt of sandal-wood and her lips of lotus.' The householder-treasure is gifted with a special kind of clairvoyance which enables him to see buried treasure whenever and wherever the king may happen to be in need of gold. And the councillor-treasure is 'wise, experienced, clever and competent to advise the King on how to proceed with what should be proceeded with, and to withdraw from what should be withdrawn from, and to overlook what should be overlooked.'[9]

These fairy-tale gifts are not as arbitrary or fantastic as they may at first appear. Traditionally they are identified with the seven factors of Enlightenment. The wheel, on this interpretation, would represent mindfulness, the fundamental quality of wakefulness, awareness, here-and-nowness of the mind; the elephant, with his sensitive and probing trunk, represents investigation, the ability to probe, analyse, test, look into things; the flying horse is energy or vigour; the jewel is joy, the mental and physical energization that gives interest, liveliness and zest to our thoughts and actions; the woman-treasure, the queen, is tranquillisation or steadying; the householder, the one who can find treasure everywhere, is concentration, whose fullest form is the deep stillness of meditation; and the counsellor, the one who tells the king what to do and what to leave undone, is equanimity: the even or balanced mind which is not swayed erratically this way or that, not biased in its judgments. The more we reflect on these images the more appropriate they seem, and we can see that they are the things to be treasured and cultivated not only by a mythical king but by anyone who wishes for balance, practical competence and a degree of profundity in life.

And perhaps partly for this reason, the King, we are told, has four special qualities: first, he is handsome, good to look at, pleasing; secondly, he is long-lived, outliving other men; thirdly, he is free from illness; and fourthly, he is beloved and popular with both Brahmins and householders, so that when he passes by with his army, the people come and beg him, 'Pass slowly by, Sire, that we may see you as long as possible.'

But the Great King not only *has* things, he also *does* things. He constructs lotus-ponds for his people—in ancient India this would be thought of as both beautifying the landscape and providing a public service, for the ponds would provide water for washing and so on. The lotus-ponds are described in detail and form the basis for another kaleidoscopic vision of a kind with which we are now familiar:

> the lotus ponds were lined with tiles of four colours, gold, silver, beryl and crystal, each pond being approached by four staircases, one gold, one silver, one beryl and one crystal. And the gold staircase had gold posts with silver railings and banisters, the silver staircase had silver posts with gold railings and banisters;[10]

well, you can imagine the rest. But it must be stressed that these descriptions are not simply some form of meaningless time-wasting repetition. Listening to them in full, one finds a rhythm build up; and we should remember that these texts were originally not written down but chanted. In one sense, we are listening to a series of musical variations; in another, to a magical ritual which involves the mind more and more deeply in a shining visionary world which expands and refreshes the consciousness before bringing it back, enlivened and purified, to the world of everyday reality (which, of course, it is the task of that consciousness to nurture and where necessary to change). Reading these passages in the great Buddhist *suttas* one is irresistibly reminded of certain passages in the major poems of William Blake:

> And every minute has an azure tent with silken veils,
> And every hour has a bright golden gate guarded with skill,
> And every day & night has walls of brass and gates of adamant,
> Shining like precious stones and ornamented with appropriate
>   signs;
> And every month a silver-paved terrace builded high,
> And every year invulnerable barriers with high towers,
> And every age is moated deep with bridges of silver & gold . . .[11]

The vision is a universal cosmic vision, and we should perhaps think of these jewels and precious metals not as the heavy minerals we know in ordinary life but as elements of pure colour and light.

Let us return to King Mahasudassana. Having provided the lotus ponds, he has them planted with lotus flowers so that the people may make garlands; he places bathing attendants on the sides of the pools so that the people may bathe; he establishes charitable distributions of food, drink, clothes, transport, sleeping-places and money for those who are poor and have none; and even marriage-brokers, so that those in need of a marriage-partner can be taken care of. Now, it is clear that none of this could last even a week if the people were to exploit it as cynically as we might expect most modern populations to do. But this text offers an ideal of citizenship as well as of kingship. For the prosperous Brahmins and householders gather together great wealth and go to offer it to the King, saying 'Sire, here is wealth that we have gathered together especially for your majesty, please accept it.' Here we have an ideal, perhaps, of taxation as a gift-relationship, offered as a present rather than painfully extorted; and it gets better, for the King replies, 'Thank you, friends, but I have enough wealth from legitimate revenues. Let this be yours, and take away more besides.'[12]

Now the citizens reflect that it would not be right for them to take the money back again. They decide to use it in building a dwelling for the King. At this point in the text, one can see the possibility of coming full-circle: are we going to get another structure with seven walls, built out of seven kinds of gems, with four gates and so on and so forth? Indeed we do, but first there is an interesting switch of levels. The King agrees that his subjects may build him a palace, and we are told 'then Sakka [another name for the Hindu god Indra], king of the gods, knowing in his mind King Mahasudassana's thought, said to his attendant god Visakamma, 'Come, friend Visakamma, and build a dwelling-place for King Mahasudassana, a palace called Dhamma.' The focus now, in short, is on the spiritual realm; whatever the citizens may be doing in the material realm, we are now looking at something which corresponds to it on a higher plane. On the basis of his inner and outer qualities and actions, the gods are now building for the King the Palace of Dhamma: the palace of what is Right, the palace of cosmic law, the palace of profound spiritual truth. And now come the gold, silver, beryl and crystal, the staircases with gold posts with silver railings and banisters and so on, which recur in this text like the refrain to an enormous song, giving a sense of the cosmic cycles revolving. (And here, too, we can see the appropriateness of the image of the wheel, for it is the wheel of the cosmos, the wheel of time itself, always changing but always the same, which is now turning around the King). And, as always, there are new details: the palace of Dhamma has eighty-four thousand chambers. In the gold chamber was a silver couch, in the silver chamber was a gold couch, in the beryl chamber was an ivory couch, and in the crystal chamber was a sandalwood couch. On the door of the gold chamber a gold palm tree was figured, with golden trunk, leaves and fruit; on the door of the silver chamber a silver palm tree was figured, with silver trunk, leaves and fruit . . . and all around the outside are the golden and silver bells, to which the gamblers and drunkards dance.

There is a quality about all this, expanded as it were to symphonic scale, which one recognises from the fairy-tales of one's childhood: those repetitious riddling fragments of verse, half nonsense and half very profound sense, which come round again and again in the old fairy-tales and ballads. They are the incantations that, while we may feel that they lull us to sleep, actually awaken another part of our minds to the truth that we find ourselves in an intangible present moment which is actually just one facet in the surface of an immense spiritual process of which we are normally unconscious, and whose scale would both intoxicate and appal us if we saw it as a whole. It is possible, indeed, that we human beings, entranced in our everyday concerns and dangerously heedless of our mortality, yet still delighting to hear these stories from a deeper world, are in a sense the 'drunkards and gamblers' who dance so cheerfully to the music which comes from the outermost fringes of these great myths.

But to return to the palace of Dhamma. As in so many legends, notably of course the great western myth embodied in the Grail legend, it is important for the hero to ask a question. And King Mahasudassana does just that. He asks himself, 'As a result of what karma is it the result, that I am now so mighty and powerful?' And he realises, 'It is the fruit, of the result, of three kinds of karma: of giving, of self-control, and of abstinence.' And with that thought, the King goes to the great gabled chamber and, standing at the threshold, exclaims: 'May the thought of lust cease! May the thought of ill-will cease! May the thought of cruelty cease! Thus far and no further the thought of lust, of ill-will, of cruelty!'[13] And he goes into the great gabled chamber, and sits down cross-legged on the golden couch, and, 'detached from all sense-desires, detached from unwholesome mental states,' he enters into meditation, passing from one level of meditation to another until he reaches the fourth and deepest level of meditation. Then, emerging from the meditation and from the great gabled chamber which perhaps symbolises it, he goes to the great golden chamber, and seated cross-legged on the silver couch, pervades first one quarter of the world, then the second, and so on, with a mind filled with loving-kindness, radiating love and goodwill to all beings in each direction in turn. And then he does the same with a mind filled with compassion, with rejoicing in the joys of others, and finally with equanimity.

The final episode in King Mahasudassana's story is an unexpected one. It conveys the sense that we are suddenly awakening from a dream, perhaps a dream which has lasted for many lifetimes. There is also, apparently, the implication that at the time when these events take place the human life-span was far longer than it is now. For, we are told, 'After many hundred, many hundred thousand years, the Queen Subhadda thought, "it is a long time since I saw King Mahasudassana. Suppose I were to go and see him?" '[14] And she sets out with her retinue to the Palace of Dhamma to see the King. When the King learns of her approach, he has the gold couch brought out and set amongst the gold palm trees, and lies down on it. When the Queen sees him, we are told that she thinks 'King Mahasudassana's faculties are purified, his complexion is clear and bright, oh—I hope he is not dead!' And when she comes close to him, she proceeds to remind him of all his fabulous wealth and his royal possessions in the hope of making him wish to stay alive. The King's response is unexpected: 'For a long time, O Queen,' he says, 'You spoke pleasing, delightful, attractive words to me; but now your words have been unpleasing, undelightful, unattractive to me.' 'Sire, ' says the Queen, 'how then am I to speak to you?'

The King's reply is:

You should speak thus: 'All things that are pleasing and attractive are liable to change, to vanish, to become otherwise. Do not, Sire, die filled with longing. To die filled with longing is painful and blameworthy. Of your eighty-four thousand cities, Kusavati is the chief: abandon desire, abandon the longing to live there . . .'[15]

At this, the Queen first of all weeps, but then she begins to speak as the King has requested, reminding him of all his royal possessions and exhorting him to abandon attachment and desire to each of them in turn. The King then dies happily and calmly, and, we are told, is reborn in the Brahma-world.

Now comes the final surprise. We must recall that this whole story is being told by the elderly Buddha to his disciple Ananda. 'Now, Ananda,' he concludes, 'You might think that King Mahasudassana at that time was somebody else. But you should not regard it so, for I was King Mahasudassana then. Those eighty-four thousand cities of which Kusavati was the chief were mine . . .'[16] and so on. The Buddha, it turns out, has been recalling one of his own past lives; and the small, out of the way town where he will pass away is the former capital, after some inconceivably vast epoch, of what was then his own great empire. Indeed, he tells Ananda, no less than seven times he has ruled as a great king in this place. But now he will pass away as a Buddha, and there will be no eighth time for him.

Let us sum up what we have so far learned about the Wheel-Turning King. He is a king whose predominance comes above all from his inner nature. The great wheel arises as a sign of his readiness to perform religious observance and as a mark of his contemplative spirit, his willingness to turn inward in contemplation. It is accompanied by the other treasures of thoughtful investigation, energy, joy, tranquillity, concentration and equanimity. He conquers the surrounding realms—in other words, achieves ascendancy over them—by his own good qualities, by reminding their inhabitants of fundamental moral laws and by his friendly tolerance and generosity. He is generous to his citizens and cares especially for the needs of the poor. As a result they regard him with great affection, and return his generosity. His palace is, above all, the palace of Dhamma. He enjoys his possessions and his power, but he also knows when and how to let go of them. And there is the suggestion that his life as a monarch may, in a sense, be an important stage of preparation for a future spiritual role.

This, briefly sketched, is the ideal of kingship as set out in the Pali texts, dating from perhaps 500 BC and written down around AD 100. But things can go wrong. How badly, indeed catastrophically wrong they can go, is indicated in a companion text, the Cakavattisihanadasutta. The title of this text means 'The Lion's Roar on the Turning of the Wheel'. The 'Lion's Roar' is a title assigned to a number of important teachings given by the Buddha, and it is clear that in this case the wheel which turns is above all that of time or history, as we shall see.

The story in this sutta is a little different. Once again we are introduced to a wheel-turning king. As before he is a righteous Dhamma-king, a conqueror of the four quarters, who has established the security of his realm and possesses the seven treasures. But there is a different perspective on the ending of his reign. You will remember that the great wheel came to rest on the royal palace, as an adornment. Now the King, we are told, sets a man to keep an eye on it, and to report to him if the wheel should slip from its position. Eventually it does so and the man goes to tell the King. The King then knows that the end of his life is approaching. Here again the story is a little different, for once he knows this, he sends for his son, installs him as king, and goes off to the forest as a royal sage to lead the contemplative life for the days that remain to him. Here, then, the transition from king to wandering ascetic is, in a way, compressed into a single lifetime—following, in fact, the Hindu tradition of the fourth stage of life, when the elderly householder gives up his secular powers and possessions and becomes a forest-dweller.

His son, then, has ascended the throne. But seven days after his father's abdication, the wheel disappears. Deeply concerned, the new King goes after his father to ask his advice. His father's reply is important. 'My son, you should not grieve or feel sad at the disappearance of the wheel-treasure. The wheel-treasure is not an heirloom from your fathers. Now, my son, you must turn yourself into an Ariyan Wheel-Turner.'[17] And his father explains that if he performs the duties of a wheel-turning monarch, then in due course, on a full-moon day, as he goes up to the terrace of the palace to observe the fast day, then the wheel-treasure may appear for him too. Further detailed advice is given about the duties of such a king—essentially, the advice is to honour and cherish Dhamma, to have it as one's badge and banner, to establish protection for it and then to establish protection for all members of the community, even down to the birds and the beasts. And the new King proceeds to follow the advice and to do all that we have already heard that a wheel-turning king must do. And sure enough, after a time, the wheel-treasure appears to him and all happens as before. And he sets a man to keep an eye on the wheel-treasure, and one day, when it slips from its place, he knows that his days are numbered and he does as his father did. And when, after his abdication, the great wheel disappears altogether, the son goes to seek his father and asks him what to do. And so the knowledge is passed on.

Now, we observe that all these new kings, although following a pattern, have done one thing of their own initiative. The one thing is this. When the wheel disappears soon after their ascent to the throne, they have gone off to their retired father, the 'royal sage', and asked his advice about what to do. Now, after seven generations, a new king takes over from his father, and when, seven days after his coronation, the great wheel disappears, this new king, although feeling grieved at its vanishing, does not go after his father to seek advice. Instead, we are told, 'he ruled the people according to his own ideas; and being so ruled, the people did not prosper so well as they had done under the previous kings who had performed the duties of the wheel-turning monarch.' In fact, the change is so noticeable that the ministers, counsellors and Brahmins form a kind of delegation and come to the king, saying

> Sire, so long as you rule the people according to your own ideas, and differently from the way they were ruled before under previous wheel-turning monarchs, they do not prosper . . . Sire, there are [people] in your realm . . . who have preserved the knowledge of how a wheel-turning monarch ought to rule. Ask us, your majesty, and we will tell you.[18]

The King certainly has the sense to see the value of this, so he summons the wise men of the kingdom and they advise him on how to rule. And he puts into practice the ways of a wheel-turning monarch in all details—except one. He does not give property to the needy, and so poverty becomes rife. So rife does it become, in fact, that at length somebody 'takes what is not given'—in other words, commits theft. The King realises his mistake, and gives the man property. But now other poor people see that theft is rewarded, so they start to steal too. At first the King gives them too property; but at last he loses patience and has a man executed. Finding themselves threatened with violent punishment, the thieves arm themselves and begin to commit their robberies with violence. And the human life-span, which at that time had been eighty thousand years, begins to decrease . . . It shrinks to forty thousand years. And the people become less beautiful.

Now, to preserve their lives in this violent society, people start to lie. Morality degenerates, envy and malice spread. Harsh speech and idle chatter become widespread. People's sexual behaviour deteriorates: first of all adultery is committed, then incest. Men couple with men and women with women. And all the time the human life-span decreases and people become uglier. Soon the life-span is down to two hundred years, then one hundred. All this, we are told, came at first from the failure to give property to the needy. And we have not seen the worst yet.

'A time will come,' the Buddha tells his followers, 'when the children of these people will have a life-span of ten years. And with them girls will be marriageable at five years old . . . With them the ten courses of moral conduct will completely disappear, [for] there will be no word for 'moral', so how can there be anyone who acts in a moral way? Those people who have no respect for mother or father, for ascetics and Brahmins, for the head of the clan, will be the ones who enjoy honour and prestige.'[19] Still worse, he tells us, for those people there will come to be a yearly 'sword-week', at which time blades will appear in people's hands and it will be regarded as legitimate to kill any person one wishes. People will hide in the grassy thickets and jungle recesses and clumps of trees or inaccessible mountains, living on the roots and fruits of the forest, to escape from being killed by one another.

At this stage, the great wheel has turned to its lowest point. Dhamma has been forgotten and men are far worse than beasts. But some people will not wish to kill or be killed. They will emerge from the trees at the end of the week glad to see one another still alive, and will resolve that the killing should not continue. They will abstain from the taking of life, and will find that their life-span and beauty increase somewhat. The precept against killing will, in other words, have been rediscovered. Little by little, over a long time-span, others will follow as the wheel of time slowly revolves and, with their own efforts to turn it, caries them upwards again . . . Theft will be seen to be wrong. Lying and drunkenness will be disapproved. And at last, when the human condition has again become civilised and the human life-span has returned to one hundred years, the next Buddha, Maitreiya the Buddha of Loving-Kindness, will be born in the world, once again to teach the Dhamma in all its fullness. The moral drawn by the Buddha for his monks is simply this: 'keep to your own preserves, monks; keep to your ancestral haunts.'[20] In other words, continue to live by the teachings and traditions you have inherited. Ask for guidance from the wise before it is too late. Live according to Dhamma, not according to your own ideas. Cherish the teachings and practices which have served you well in the past.

A few words to sum up. The myth of the wheel-turning monarch is a teaching for lay-people. As the Buddha is in one sense the ideal figure of the religious ascetic, so the *Cakkavatti* King is the ideal of the lay person, the householder. The legend shows how one with possessions, children, a house, money, and worldly duties, some or all of these, may live rightly and benefit the world. It shows that power must grow out of goodness, and be yielded to voluntarily by those who come under it. It shows that relationships must be based on generosity. It stresses that there is nothing inherently wrong with riches; for the layman to be prosperous is appropriate, but those riches must be used with generosity and given up readily when the time comes. It demonstrates that inner qualities lead to outer success, and that both must be based on Dhamma—on the sacred laws and traditions of the cosmos—and that we must be ready ourselves to ask for advice from the wise, without waiting for that advice to be thrust upon us. It shows the part played by the lay person in maintaining the order of the world; and it suggests that neglect of the poorest and weakest may be the crucial oversight which can lead to the destruction of human society.

Above all it shows the monarch as a symbol of qualities to which all may aspire, and as a secular figure who nonetheless makes the spiritual life possible for himself and others. By living the worldly life in accordance with Dhamma, the wheel-turning monarch becomes a guardian of tradition and the cosmic order for the benefit of all.

NOTES

1. Walshe 451–2, 457 (RD II, 154, 162). All the *suttas* cited in this paper are available in translation in two standard versions: *The Long Discourses of the Buddha: A Translation of the Digha Nikaya*, tr. Maurice Walshe (Boston, Mass.: Wisdom Publications, 1997), hereafter cited as Walshe; and *Dialogues of the Buddha: Translated from the Pali of the Digha Nikaya*, tr. T. W. and C. A. F. Rhys Davids, 3 vols (London: Pali Text Society, 1910 (fourth edition 1977)), hereafter cited as RD. In the present paper the texts as quoted are generally taken from Walshe, with occasional adjustments of wording; references to RD follow in brackets.

2. Walshe 457 (RD II, 162).
3. Walshe 279 (RD II, 199–200).
4. Walshe 279–80 (RD II, 200).
5. Walshe 280 (RD II, 201).
6. RD II, 201–2 (cf. Walshe 280).
7. Walshe 280 (RD II, 202).

8. RD II, 203 (cf. Walshe 281).

9. Walshe 282-3 (RD II, 208).

10. Walshe 283 (RD II, 210).

11. William Blake, *Milton* I 28. 50-6.

12. Walshe 284 (RD II, 211-2).

13. Walshe 286 (RD II, 218).

14. Walshe 288 (RD II, 222).

15. Walshe 289 (RD II, 225).

16. Walshe 289 (RD II, 229).

17. Walshe 396 (RD III, 61).

18. Walshe 398 (RD III, 85).

19. Walshe 401 (RD III, 70).

20. Walshe 404 (RD III, 75).

NOTES ON CONTRIBUTORS

JOHN S. ALLITT has taught Dante studies for many years, twice having lead Temenos Academy seminar groups through a reading of the complete *Divine Comedy*, and more recently giving a course of some 21 lectures on the deeper significance of Dante's great work. He is a Fellow of the Temenos Academy.

L. L. BLAKE is a barrister, author and lecturer. He has recently published *The Royal Law* concerning the language and importance of the Coronation Service. His other books include two for teenagers, *Young People's Book of the Constitution* and *Young People's Book of the Law*; and for general interest, *Sovereignty: Power Beyond Politics* and *The Prince and the Professor*.

JOHN CAREY is a lecturer in the Department of Early and Medieval Irish, National University of Ireland, Cork. He is the author of the books *King of Mysteries: Early Irish Religious Writings* and *A Single Ray of the Sun: Religious Speculation in Early Ireland*, together with many articles on the religious and intellectual culture of early Ireland. He is a member of the Council and a Fellow of the Temenos Academy.

GREVEL LINDOP is Emeritus Professor of English at Manchester University; the General Editor of the collected edition of the works of Thomas de Quincey; author of *The Opium-Eater: A Life of Thomas de Quincey*; and a distinguished poet. He teaches Buddhist meditation under the auspices of the Samatha Trust. He is the Editor of the *Temenos Academy Review* and Academic Director of the Temenos Academy.

JOSEPH MILNE has lead reading essential texts seminar groups at the Temenos Academy almost without interruption for the past ten years, mainly devoted to the study of the plays of Shakespeare. He is a Visiting Tutor to the University of Kent where he teaches on the MA Course in Mysticism and Religious Experience. He is a Fellow of the Temenos Academy.

KATHLEEN RAINE, C.B.E., the Founder of the Temenos Academy, is our most distinguished living poet and, through her advocacy of the primacy of the Imagination, a source of inspiration to many. Her *Collected Poems* was published in 2000.

LIST OF SUBSCRIBERS

Dr. Ian Addison
The Revd. A. Alexis
His Excellency Dr. Ghazi
 Algosaibi
Martin Andic
Jean Archer
Christine Baker
Stephen Barber
Anne Baring
Val Barry
Dr. Carmen Blacker
Thetis Blacker
Leslie Blake
Eric Boagey
Mark Bolland
Ambrose Boothby
Diana Borel
Juliet de Boulay
David Brazier
Louise Brocklehurst
Tony Butler
Nigel Butterley
Andrey Bykov
Prof. David Cadman
Bernard Canetti
Dr. John Carey
Jules Cashford
Julia Chalkley
Ann Chick
Elspeth Chowdharay-
 Best
Barbara Clauson
Alan Clodd
Helen Cockburn
Ann Colcord
A. T. Cole
David Coussell
Ginevra Coward
Christopher Cullen
John Cunnington
I. H. Cuss
Dr. Peter Davies
Olivia Dewhurst-
 Maddock

C. P. Douglas
Tom Durham
The School of Economic
 Science
S. Elkes
Richard Emanuel
Kathleen Evans
Rouksana Fakim
A. D. Farndell
P. Farndell
James Fisher
Graham Fletcher
M. Fox
Dr. Hans-Wolfgang Frick
Margaret Frost
J. C. Garvey
Jacqueline Gerry
Christopher Gibbs
Costantino Giorgetti
Timothy Glazier
Philip Goldsmith
Martha Grossman
Dr. R. Gupta
Dr. Hans Hakl
P. Hall
Susan Hannis
Charles Hardaker
Patrick Harpur
Carol Hartley
Dr. Christopher Hay,
 Marquis de Vaux-
 Balthi, KGCOSJ
Jean Head
Justin Hedley
Steve Higgins
Dick Hill
Prof. Jeremy Hooker
Tony Horner
Diane Howard
Esme Howard
Howard Hull
P. F. Hull
Marie Ingram

Peter Jewell
Brian Keeble
Matt Kittay
Vasant Kothari
Carl Laubin
Christine Laubin
Adrian Leigh
Esmond Lindop
Prof. Grevel Lindop
Jill Line
Richard Lines
David Lorimer
Annabel Lubikowski
Jennifer Madden
Christine Maddox
Manubhai Madhvani
Chris Malcomson
John Matthews
Claire McCall
S. M. Minhinnick
Diane Mooney
Anthony Murphy
Joyce Musson
Jacinta Nadal
Helen Neale
Helen Newman
Sean O'Hagan
Lufthi O'Meagher
Genevieve Overy
Stephen Overy
Geoffrey Parkes
Vivien Piercy
Annabel Pitt
Norman Pope
Todd Pratum
Zara Quensel
Valerie Rees
Alan Roberts
Caroline Robinson
The Lady Romsey
James Roose-Evans
Nomi Rowe
R. M. Rowett

Juliet Salaman
Verity Saunders
Michael Schneider
Gay Schroeder
Brian Scott-McCarthy
Justine Scott-McCarthy
Susan Scrimgeour
Lindy Seago
Tim Seago
Anne Seward
R. C. A. Shaw
Michael Shepherd
Susan Sheridan
Ian Skelly
Dr. Nancy Smith
Alexandra Stainow
Robert Stannard
Nancy Stone
Stephen Stuart-Smith
Elza Tantcheva
Andrew Tatham
Ruth Templeton
Katherine Tetlow
Janet Todhunter
Jennifer Turnbull
Philippa Vaughan
Andrew Vernede
Douglas Verrall
Emma Vickers
S. M. Wade
Susan Walker
Diana Walls
Bruno Wang
Rosemary Warner
The Ven. John Weaver
Pamela, The Lady
 Wedgwood
Dr. Karel Werner
C. A. Wild
Simon Windsor-Clive
Dr. Duncan Wu
Dr. H. Zuberi

The Temenos Academy is a registered charity
which aims to offer education in philosophy and the arts
in the light of the sacred traditions of East and West, through
lecture and seminar courses, publications and audio tapes.

For further information please write to:
The Temenos Academy, P.O. Box 203, Ashford, Kent TN25 5ZT.